STANDARD LOAN

UNLESS RECALLED BY ANOTHER READER
THIS ITEM MAY BE BORROWED FOR

FOUR WEEKS

To renew
01243 81
01243 812(

Tea
Ear

This practical and accessible book explores ways of developing continuity and coherence in children's learning from three to seven years old. It is based around three case studies in which tutors on Initial Teacher Training courses worked with Early Years practitioners in three different pre-school settings, each linked to a primary school. The book describes how they successfully managed to plan and teach integrated themes across the age-range in the context of the requirements of the Foundation Stage and the National Curriculum.

Each case study has a different focus:

- science, design and technology
- 'the arts' – including an ICT strand
- 'the humanities' – including a physical education strand

English and mathematics dimensions run through each theme. The book is alive with discussion of children's art, language, drama and music, captured as field notes, writing, drawing, and as video tape. Each chapter concludes with suggestions of ways in which readers can develop the ideas in their own contexts.

This book will be invaluable reading for students on Early Years courses, for Early Years practitioners, and tutors and mentors in early childhood education.

Hilary Cooper is Reader in Education at St Martin's College, Lancaster. Her previous publications include *Children's Perceptions of Learning with Trainee Teachers* (2000) and *Teaching History in the Early Years*, 2nd Edition (2002), both published by RoutledgeFalmer.
Chris Sixsmith is a Principal Lecturer at St Martin's College, Lancaster.

UNIVERSITY
COLLEGE
CHICHESTER
LIBRARY

372.
21
C OO

WS 2199749 7

04/04   TES

Teaching across the Early Years 3–7

Curriculum Coherence and Continuity

Edited by
Hilary Cooper and
Chris Sixsmith

RoutledgeFalmer
Taylor & Francis Group

LONDON AND NEW YORK

First published 2003 by RoutledgeFalmer
11 New Fetter Lane, London EC4P 4EE

Simultaneously published in the USA and Canada
by RoutledgeFalmer
29 West 35th Street, New York, NY 10001

RoutledgeFalmer is an imprint of the Taylor & Francis Group

© 2003 Hilary Cooper and Chris Sixsmith, selection and editorial
matter; individual chapters, the contributors

Typeset in Sabon by
Florence Production Ltd, Stoodleigh, Devon.
Printed and bound in Great Britain by
TJ International Ltd, Padstow, Cornwall

All rights reserved. No part of this book may be reprinted
or reproduced or utilised in any form or by any electronic,
mechanical, or other means, now known or hereafter invented,
including photocopying and recording, or in any information
storage or retrieval system, without permission in writing
from the publishers.

British Library Cataloguing in Publication Data
A catalogue record for this book is available from the
British Library

Library of Congress Cataloguing in Publication Data
A catalog record for this book has been requested

ISBN 0–415–25472–8 (hbk)
ISBN 0–415–25473–6 (pbk)

UNIVERSITY COLLEGE CHICHESTER LIBRARIES

AUTHOR:

TITLE: S NO.

                                    372·21 COO

DATE: SUBJECT:
        APRIL 04   TES

For the early years educator, therefore, the process of education – how children learn – is as important as, and inseparable from, the content – what children learn. We believe that this principle must underlie all curriculum planning for the under fives.

(The Rumbold Report)

DES (1990) *Starting with Quality: A Report of the Committee of Enquiry into the Quality of Educational Experiences Offered to 3–4 Year Olds* (The Rumbold Report), London: HMSO.

Contents

List of figures

List of tables

ST MARK'S DAY CARE UNIT PLAYGROUP AND MARKET GATES INFANTS' SCHOOL

List of contributors

Andrea Brook is a lecturer in art education at St Martin's College. She has taught extensively in primary schools, both in England and abroad. Her previous post was that of art coordinator in a large international school in Vienna. She is particularly interested in the ways in which children learn through art.

Christine Cooper is a senior lecturer in history at St Martin's College, where she teaches mainly on Early Years courses. She has considerable experience of teaching young children and is particularly interested in the links between history and literacy. Her main research interest is the impact of government policies on practice in schools.

Hilary Cooper is reader in Education at St Martin's College. Previously she lectured in education at Goldsmiths College, London. She taught young children for many years; her doctoral research was undertaken as a practising class teacher. She has published widely.

Liz Elliott is a senior lecturer in education and information and communication technology at St Martin's College, which includes both the advanced study of Early Years and ICT as its specialist options. She spent a number of years in primary schools as an Early Years teacher and ICT coordinator and has provided ICT courses for teachers and parents. Her M.Sc research was concerned with the cognitive psychology of how young children learn new skills. She is particularly interested in the effects of high self-esteem on children's learning.

Owain Evans is responsible for Year 2 students on the BA (Hons)/QTS course on the Ambleside campus of St Martin's College and is course leader for design and technology throughout the college. These roles bring him into regular contact with Early Years trainees and Early Years practitioners. As a head teacher he encouraged cross-phase liaison and collaborative teaching

Margaret Foster has many years' experience of working in schools with responsibility for the Foundation Stage and Key Stage 1. She has also taught in a special school, a college of further education and on university teacher education courses.

Robin Foster has taught in primary schools and in higher education where he has had responsibility for mathematics education.

Kevin Hamel is the music resource and development officer for Cumbria Learning Support Service. He is a visiting lecturer in music and education at Lancaster University, and coordinates an innovative primary curriculum support website (www.tuned-in.org).

Kirsty Klijn is a class teacher at Stramongate Primary School, Kendal. She is a music specialist and coordinates music throughout the school.

Katharine Langley-Hamel is a senior lecturer in English in primary education at St Martin's College Ambleside campus.

Jim Lavin is a principal lecturer and head of programme for physical education at St Martin's College. In his doctoral research he investigated the impact of the National Curriculum on the practice of physical education in primary schools. His research interests include the social and cooperative aspects of the teaching of physical education.

Lisa Melbourne currently teaches the nursery class and is the science co-ordinator at Ingleton Primary School in Yorkshire. She has extensive experience of teaching reception-age children and has also taught in Key Stages 1 and 2.

Pete Saunders is leader of educational information and communication courses at the Ambleside campus of St Martin's College. Previously he was Eastern Region coordinator of the National Primary Project, part of the government's Microelectronics Education Programme.

Neil Simco is dean of the Faculty of Education at St Martin's College, where he has responsibility for a large portfolio of programmes leading to the award of Qualified Teacher Status. His subject specialism is geography. He has published extensively in the fields of primary education and primary teacher education.

Chris Sixsmith is a principal lecturer in primary education at St Martin's College, Ambleside campus. He has had considerable experience of teaching three- to seven-year-olds both in England and in Tanzania. He lectured in psychology and early childhood education at Edge Hill College and Charlotte Mason College.

Nigel Toye is senior lecturer in drama at St Martin's College. He works with trainee teachers on primary and secondary courses. He is co-author, with Francis Prendiville, of *Drama in Traditional Story for the Early Years* and continues to research the use of teacher-in-role as a strategy for promoting effective learning.

Acknowledgements

Our project aims to celebrate and support the ongoing and often under-valued efforts of Early Years practitioners. They still find time and energy to liaise with each other and to create meaningful and exciting learning environments for the children with whom they work, while also meeting the demands of National Curriculum guidance and statutory requirements. We are immeasurably grateful to those who agreed to participate in the project. They made the time to discuss their work with us, to share their planning with us (and so with you). They allowed colleagues from college to work with them in their classrooms on focused aspects of their plans, to write about these sessions and to record them on videotape as a basis for further discussion.

In our account the names of the schools, teachers and children have been changed, but we hope that their voices, and a feel for the varied environments in which they work, will shine through, for they are very real people in very real places. We should especially like to thank Dawn Harvey, head teacher of Ingleton Primary School, and members of her staff: Alison Capstick, Lisa Melbourne, Kate Rowe and Gillian Walton. Lisa Melbourne, the nursery class teacher at Ingleton Primary School, is also co-author, with Chris Sixsmith, of Chapter 2.

We are grateful to Peter Sloan, head teacher of Stramongate Primary School and to the members of his staff who worked with us on the project: the reception class teachers, Sue Carr and Sue Moratto-Smith; Linda Fletcher, the deputy head teacher, and Linda Horsman, who teach Year 1 classes; Pat Etches and Fran Elliott who teach Year 2 classes. We are especially grateful to Kirsty Klijn, who teaches Year 3. Kirsty coordinated the project in Stramongate and is the author of Chapter 6. Our thanks are also due to Sue Matthews, head teacher of Brantfield Nursery School and her staff, and especially to the nursery teacher, Veronica Broyd.

We are grateful to Anne Desforges, head teacher of Deepdale Infants School, and to the members of her staff who worked with us: Helen Usher, Pru Lee, Pat Horsfield, Anne Healey and Dympna Mooney. We should like to pay tribute to Jean Utting, director of St Luke's social services day care unit, to her deputy, Sandra Simpson, and to the nursery officers, Monica Tipper, Anne McHale and Fiona Beetham.

We, the editors, would also like to express our appreciation to colleagues in college who agreed to take part in the project and to contribute chapters to this book. They all teach on Early Years Initial Teacher Training courses and other courses preparing practitioners to work with young children in school and pre-school settings. Between them they have subject expertise which spans the curriculum. They manage to retain their enthusiasm and belief in their work despite heavy workloads and the need to respond to rigorous external pressures. And they still found time to attend meetings, work with children and teachers, write their chapters, meet deadlines (well, almost), accept editorial suggestions with good humour and revise drafts. Thank you.

Our thanks also to other colleagues: Samantha Twiselton, senior lecturer in English in primary education, for her involvement in Chapter 10, and to Chris Rowley, senior lecturer in geography, who advised on aspects of Part 2. Also to Michael Holloway of Spindlewood Publishers for the UK of 'Nnenna and her Udara Tree' from *Isimeme's Stories* by Isimeme Ibazebo.

Finally, all those who enjoyed working together on the project over the past year, who believed in it, wanted it to succeed and eventually to share it with others, owe a debt of gratitude to Marion Blake. Marion has a good deal of experience in the worlds of education and publishing, so we were delighted when she agreed to act as our freelance consultant. She read our drafts, commented on them and gave us clear guidance on how to develop them, often during late-night telephone conversations. Now we hope that our book reflects our individual voices but also has a consistent style. We wanted it to read like a story, with conversations into which busy colleagues might be drawn even at the end of a hard day, a real story in which they may hear resonances of their own day. We hope that you, the readers, will want to develop the story in your own contexts. This is the vision given to us by Marion. Only you will be able to tell us whether we have succeeded.

Hilary Cooper and Chris Sixsmith

References are made throughout the book to the following documents, published by the Department for Education and Employment and the Qualifications and Curriculum Authority:

1998   *The National Literacy Framework for Teaching*
1999   *The National Curriculum for Key Stages 1 and 2: Handbook for Primary Teachers in England*
2000   *Curriculum Guidance for the Foundation Stage*
2000   *Music Teachers' Guide*
2001   *Planning, Teaching and Assessing the Curriculum for Pupils with Learning Difficulties: Developing Skills*

Chapter 1

Mapping out the project: aims, rationale, organization

Hilary Cooper and Chris Sixsmith

The Owl and the Pussy-cat went to sea
In a beautiful, pea-green boat,
They took some honey, and plenty of money,
Wrapped up in a five-pound note . . .
They sailed away, for a year and a day,
To the land where the Bong-tree grows . . .
                        (*Edward Lear*, 'The Owl and the Pussy-cat')

The £5000 allocated by the college research committee to 'explore ways of developing coherence and continuity in the Early Years education of three-to-seven-year-olds was not exactly 'plenty of money', but it was sufficient, and the journey lasted almost exactly 'a year and a day'. But here our story diverges from that of the Owl and the Pussy-cat, for there was no romantic tryst and we did not, as far as we know, meet 'a pig with a ring in the end of his nose' or 'the turkey who lives on the hill'. Yet our search for 'the land where the Bong-tree grows' was nevertheless a search for that magical place where fantasy and imagination, fairy stories, nonsense rhymes and riddles merge with curiosity, questioning and attempts to observe and understand the real world, which adults delight in as much as children, and where they see their role as helping the children to make sense of it. It is a land first charted by the pioneers of Early Years education: Jean-Jacques Rousseau, Friedrich Froebel, Maria Montessori, Margaret and Rachel McMillan and Susan Isaacs.

Nor was our boat occupied solely by the Owl and the Pussy-cat. (Who could they be, anyway?) It was crewed by thirteen colleagues from St Martin's College employed in a variety of specialisms training students to work with young children as teachers, teaching assistants and nursery nurses, together with numerous teachers in our partnership schools who support our students' school-based work. We had all originally been inspired to want to work with young children by 'the pioneers'.

THE PIONEERS OF EARLY YEARS EDUCATION

Historically, the traditional view of childhood was that children were simply miniature adults who learned in the same way that adults learned, thought in the same way that adults thought and had the same goals and aspirations as adults. Learning was viewed as merely the acquisition of information passed on from the previous generation. No one considered the possibility that children might think and learn in a different way from adults; learning was simply a matter of the passive reception of knowledge. Not until the mid eighteenth century was this theory challenged.

Jean-Jacques Rousseau

One of the first people to do so was Jean-Jacques Rousseau, born in Geneva in 1712. Rousseau held radical views that ran counter to the received wisdom of the day. He proposed the idea that man was naturally good and all children born free from sin, and that the preservation of this innocence and virtue was central to the education process. Such ideas ran counter to the teachings of the Christian Church, which held all human beings to 'be born in sin'. He developed the concept of a 'naturally civilized man' who would create a moral society. In 1762 he published Émile, which described in detail the education of a 'modern child' based on the premises that learning is a natural process, that the young child is biologically programmed to learn particular things at particular times, and that the adult's role is to provide an environment where this learning can take place. A central tenet of the book is that children learn through personal experience: the 'complete abandonment of the pre-determined curriculum. Émile was to be educated entirely through activities and first-hand experience.' Rousseau emphasized the importance of education being based on a study of the child and the provision of experience through the senses, family life and bodily exercise rather than on rote 'book knowledge'.

Friedrich Froebel

Friedrich Froebel developed these ideas further. Born in 1782 in Germany, son of a Lutheran minister, he lost his mother at nine months old, an event he was later to view as having conditioned 'my whole future development'. His father was by all accounts a severe man whom the young Froebel feared, and he later referred to this unhappy childhood as his 'gloomy, lowering dawn'. At the age of ten he went to live with his uncle, and five years later was apprenticed to a forester. This was to prove a significant phase of his life, one where he developed his general feeling for the unity of nature and an almost mystical appreciation of the relationship between man and the natural world. In 1805 he took up his first teaching appointment but left after two years. Having set up his first school in November 1816, he went on, in 1840, to found the German *Kindergarten*, the very name of which emphasizing his belief in the links between child development and the natural world.

Froebel believed an 'eternal law' ruled all that happened. This law expressed itself in nature and also in the mind and spirit of man. Man's purpose was to 'reveal the divine element within him by allowing it to become freely effective in his life'. The role of education was to develop the child's essential nature, allowing him or her to perceive the divine as it is manifested in our natural surroundings. He felt that education should be 'permissive and following, guarding and protecting only; it should neither direct nor determine nor infer'. This belief has a direct implication for the way in which children should be educated: they should be allowed to seek the understanding of the divine without the explicit direction of adults.

> To young plants and animals we give space and time, knowing that then they will grow correctly according to inherent law. . . . But the human being is regarded as a piece of wax or a lump of clay which can be moulded into any shape we choose.
>
> (Froebal 1974: 8)

He held that five elements were essential for healthy growth:

- *Self-activity*. Children are self-active if they are doing what they feel is important, playing, imitating, carrying out their own choice of activities rather than having other people's ideas imposed on them.
- *Connectedness and unbroken continuity*. Froebel argued that there are no distinct domains of knowledge. The school should take a wide view of the curriculum. Part of the child's development is to make connections between different areas and form a unified view of the world.
- *Creativity*. Creative growth takes place when there is disequilibrium resolved by creating a new understanding.
- *Physical activity*. Froebel viewed the child as comprising mind, soul and body.
- *Happy and harmonious surroundings*. This is in general keeping with the idea of unity and equilibrium, a situation he attempted to create in his kindergartens.

Two alternative views of how children learn and develop seemed to be emerging. On the one hand there was the traditional view that children were passive recipients of knowledge – that their role was simply to absorb the information, learn the skill and develop the understanding presented to them. This was in keeping with the approach adopted in the education of older children and university students. Students, for example, were seen to be 'reading for a degree', an activity whereby they presumably absorbed the thoughts and knowledge of those who had gone before. The second view was that the young were active learners in whom the capacity for learning was inborn. Learning was a natural process, one that would unfold as the child matured providing he or she was allowed to engage with the environment in appropriate ways and was not impeded in this process by adult interference.

Maria Montessori

In the early 1900s, an Italian doctor named Maria Montessori was working with children with learning difficulties in a poor area of Rome. As part of this work she spent a good deal of time observing the children and came to a number of conclusions about the learning processes of young children. She believed that children passed through sensitive periods of development in which they were particularly receptive to certain areas of learning, and that each child was born with a unique potential: development was 'the inevitable unfolding of a biological programme'.

She viewed children as active learners who needed to be in an environment that allowed their potential to be realized. Towards this end she produced what she referred to as 'didactic materials' which the children were encouraged to handle in order to complete first simple and then more complex exercises; in many ways this process allowed them to teach themselves. She also designed learning environments that contained child-sized furniture and tools. She emphasized learning through the active use of the senses and not merely through the more passive activities of reading, listening and observation.

Margaret and Rachel McMillan

At about the same time, in London, two American sisters were starting to have an influence on the practice of nursery education. Margaret and Rachel McMillan believed the school should be an extension of the home and that a close working relationship between teachers and parents was essential for the successful education of the young child. They set up classes for parents to encourage them to assist their children's development.

After Rachel's death, Margaret continued the work they had begun together. She based her work around three main ideas:

- Children need nurturing and training. Individual adult attention is important in the education of the young child.
- Schools should be linked with the home and with health care. She introduced school meals and school medical services. She also laid great emphasis on providing a learning environment that included fresh air, gardens and areas for free play.
- Nursery teachers must be well trained.

Susan Isaacs

A further significant contribution to our understanding of how young children learn was made by Susan Isaacs (1885–1948). Drawing on the work of Froebel, Melanie Klein and Freud, she developed an understanding of the importance of giving children the freedom to think, feel and relate to others. She regarded play as an essential element in enabling them to come to terms with their world and their own development, a way of escaping into a world of imagination. Play, she believed, allowed children to solve problems, and resolve fears and anxieties. They were to be encouraged to express their inner feelings in order to avoid the dangers associated with repressing them. She felt they were restricted in their learning if they were required to sit at a desk in a classroom and follow the directions of an adult; children learned best through first-hand experience and self-chosen activities, free from the constraints imposed by adults. She too viewed the nursery as an extension of the home, and she also felt children should remain in the nursery setting until the age of seven. Isaacs was clearly in favour of child-centred education, encouraging teachers to support but not interfere with children's learning.

Throughout the middle of the last century those endorsing the idea of the child as an active learner central to the learning process drew on the work of Jean Piaget to support their ideas. Perhaps the clearest and most powerful example of this was the use of Piaget's ideas by Lady Plowden to underpin the views about primary education outlined in the Plowden Report, *Children and Their Primary Schools* (1967). This report used Piagetian theory to support educational practice not only for very young children but for all primary children. Since that time, for a number of reasons (see Sixsmith and Simco 1997), this common theoretical base underpinning primary education has changed. Educational theory has apparently moved back to the position where there are two different approaches to the way we understand children's learning. One is the approach constructed by 'the pioneers': that children should be active learners at the centre of the learning process. The other, that the content of what is to be taught should be at the centre of the process and that children should be, largely, passive recipients of that content.

THE PIONEERS AND THE FOUNDATION STAGE CURRICULUM

The *Curriculum Guidance for the Foundation Stage* in many ways reflects the philosophy, research and practical experiences of 'the pioneers' and those who followed in their footsteps. It aims to promote the development of the whole child (social, emotional, physical, cognitive), to foster personal, social and emotional well-being and to develop positive attitudes towards learning. The areas of learning are seen as broad and interlinked. The ways in which children learn through play are set out on page 25 of the *Curriculum Guidance for the Foundation Stage*. In play, it says, children learn

> to explore, develop and represent learning experiences which help them to make sense of the world, to practise and build upon ideas, concepts and skills, to understand the need for rules, to work alone and alongside others, to rehearse feelings, to take risks, to think creatively, to communicate with others, to investigate and solve problems, to express fears in safe conditions.

Learning is seen as taking place at home as well as in nursery classes and playgroups, and parents are encouraged to participate in their children's learning. It is acknowledged that children are individuals and that each is different; that they develop at different rates. It is recognized that children learn by responding to the environments in which they find themselves, by observing, asking questions, investigating and exploring, physically, socially, creatively, intellectually, and that rich and stimulating environments are therefore important.

The Foundation Stage curriculum recognizes the role social interaction plays in children's learning and aims to foster social and communication skills. It also emphasizes the need for children's learning to be structured, building on what they already know, with appropriate interventions to take them forward.

THE PIONEERS AND THE NATIONAL CURRICULUM FOR KEY STAGE I

It can be claimed that the values, aims and purposes underpinning the National Curriculum (QCA/DFEE 1999: 10–38) also reflect theoretical understandings about child development and the processes of learning. There are references to holistic approaches, to promoting spiritual, moral, social and cultural development, to enhancing language and communication skills across the curriculum, to promoting self-esteem and emotional well-being, and to the development of children's sense of identity. Key skills across the curriculum include social skills and working with others.

There are fewer specific references to play and to parental involvement. However, there is a renewed emphasis on respecting individual differences and rates of development. Teachers are expected to create learning environments and a classroom ethos which gives children the confidence to express their opinions, explain their own ideas, question and investigate, and think creatively. Certainly there is a stated expectation that there will be continuity between the early learning goals of the Foundation Stage, which some children may reach during this stage, and the level descriptions of the National Curriculum.

ROCKS, WHIRLPOOLS AND STORMY WEATHER

However, in spite of the aims and values which we may identify in both the Foundation Stage guidance and the National Curriculum, and some evidence that both have their roots in our theoretical understandings of how children learn, stormy weather lies ahead when we try to negotiate a smooth passage between the two: to provide continuity and coherence in children's learning experiences. There are three main reasons for this. First, tensions are created by differences in curriculum structure. The *Curriculum Guidance for the Foundation Stage* is organized around areas of learning while the National Curriculum for Key Stage 1 is organized around subject-based programmes of study. Second, the emphasis on statutory assessment (baseline testing, Standard Attainment Tests, literacy and numeracy hours, target-setting and league tables) can undermine Key Stage 1 teachers' intuitive understanding of the ways in which children learn and the extensive body of research on which this is based. This can have a knock-on effect both on pre-school education and parents' expectations of more formal ways of organizing the curriculum. It is more likely that the format of planned learning experiences for Key Stage 1 will filter down to the Foundation Stage rather than vice versa. Third, the variety of settings in which Foundation Stage education takes place (nursery schools, nursery and reception classes in primary schools plus a variety of playgroups and nurseries) can often prevent effective liaison from the Foundation Stage to Key Stage 1.

As a result of these tensions it can be difficult to provide for curriculum coherence, continuity, progression and relevance across the Early Years and to provide a holistic education: one that encompasses children's social, emotional and cognitive needs, one that begins with their interests, experiences and questions and gives them autonomy while keeping the framework of the statutory curriculum. If a continuum between areas of learning and the Key Stage 1 curriculum is not created, the Foundation subjects (the humanities, the arts, physical education) are in danger of being marginalized and the potential for a rich and stimulating three-to-seven curriculum could be lost.

Because of these tensions some Early Years teachers have said recently that they feel demoralized and in danger of becoming mechanistic 'deliverers' of the curriculum. That is why the teachers who worked with us on this book were keen to participate.

In the words of one of them:

> We need to try to explore ways in which we can resolve these tensions. It will give us all confidence in re-establishing our professional values.

A nursery teacher felt that it would be

> an opportunity to share ideas and get involved in curriculum evaluation with colleagues in school. We always liaise over transfer but usually we only have time for the basic practicalities.

A teacher whose specialism is music was keen to extend her experience to working in music with pre-school children:

> It will be a rare opportunity to work with college tutors in our classrooms. I'd really like some new ideas for art. We seem to have so little time for it these days.

The college tutors could see advantages for themselves:

> I wonder if I could I extend the work I've been doing on teacher-in-role in the nursery to Years 1 and 2? In what ways will the older children respond differently ?

> We'd like to understand more about how children who are at the stage of emergent writing take to word processing. Can we learn more about making efficient use of natural progression?

> Can we avoid the domination of the numeracy hour? Can we find ways of developing mathematical concepts and skills as an integral part of the rest of children's learning experiences?

THE PLANNED VOYAGE OF DISCOVERY

Destination

The aims of the project were:

- For practitioners working in three different pre-school settings, each linked to a primary school, to identify key issues or concerns, from their perspectives, about the provision of continuity, coherence and quality in children's learning experiences;
- For college tutors to identify related questions of interest to them;

- For tutors and teachers to work together with children to explore both sets of questions, in focused ways that would be manageable and realistic, given everybody's existing heavy commitments;
- To evaluate how effectively the concerns had been addressed and perhaps to identify questions for further investigations.

Organization

The project was organized in three parts, one for each term during 2001. Each part lasted about four weeks. The first took place in a village first school which had a nursery class within the school. For the second study a primary school in a large town liaised with a feeder nursery school. The third involved an infants' school in the centre of a large multicultural city and a nearby playgroup that is part of a social services day care unit.

Each case study was to have a different focus. The first would be on science, and design and technology. The second would be on 'the arts' – drama, art and music – and we decided also to include an information and communication strand. The third focus would be on 'the humanities' and included a physical education strand. Although language and mathematics would run through each of the studies, we decided, given the tutors' teaching commitments, that chapters on the language and mathematics dimensions could only be included in some of the case studies.

We were hoping to plan around themes which would integrate areas of learning at the Foundation Stage and a range of subjects at Key Stage 1 to see how the same theme might be interpreted across the three-to-seven age range in terms of coherence and continuity. The three different focuses, we hoped, would allow us to develop these in a certain amount of depth, although of course information and communication technology, drama and physical development could form part of any theme. Our aim was not to suggest that a cohort of children should repeat a theme in successive years, but to try to provide examples of planning for continuity and coherence which others could use as a starting point for developing their own themes in this way.

Each of the schools involved had worked with the college over a number of years supporting students' school-based work. Personal friendships had developed, and there was a feeling of mutual trust and respect that provided a sound basis for an honest approach to identifying concerns, working together in classrooms and evaluating outcomes.

First of all the editors, the college tutors managing the project, met the schools' head teachers and the director of the day care unit and explained how we hoped to organize the project. The teachers and those working in the pre-school setting were asked to decide on a broad theme which would fit in with their existing medium-term plans, which could be developed across the three-to-seven age range and reflected the focus for their case study:

science, the arts or the humanities. A date was agreed, several weeks ahead, when they would let the college tutors know the theme they had chosen and when they would send copies of their planning. Then each of the college tutors and all the teachers involved in the case study met in the school at the end of a day. The meetings were informal, a chance to meet each other or renew acquaintances and spark off ideas for developing work together. By the end of each meeting:

- Teachers had identified the issues they wanted to investigate;
- Tutors had talked about their own questions;
- The timescale during which teachers would work on the agreed theme had been agreed;
- It was agreed that each tutor would work for at least one focused session on an aspect of the theme with each class across the three-to-seven age range. Individual tutors would liaise with the teachers about how they would plan their work together and about mutually convenient times.

We hope that everyone with an interest in the education of three-to-seven-year-olds will find reflections of their own experiences in our book and perhaps discover that some of their questions or concerns were also ours. We hope they will take the same delight as we did in the children and the work we describe and that they will take some of our ideas further. *Bon voyage!*

BIBLIOGRAPHY

Bruce, T. and Meggit, C. (1999) *Child Care and Education* (second edition), London: Hodder & Stoughton

Curtis, A.M. (1986) *A Curriculum for the Pre-School Child*, London: NFER Nelson.

Froebal, F. (1974) *The Education of Man*, Clifton: Augustus M. Kelly.

Jackson, D. (1993) *New Approaches to Child Care*, London: Paragon.

Lilley, I.M. (1967) *Friedrich Froebel*, Cambridge: Cambridge University Press.

Department of Education and Science (1967) *The Plowden Report: Children and their Primary Schools*. Central Advisory Council for Education (England). London: HMSO.

Rousseau, J.-J. (1911) *Émile*, London: Dent.

Sixsmith, S.C. and Simco, N.P. (1997) 'The role of formal and informal theory in the training of student teachers' in *Mentoring and Tutoring* 5 (1), 4–13.

Standing, E.M. (1962) *Maria Montessori: Her Life and Work*, New York: American Library.

Part I

Dalesview First School: books, stories and rhymes

Table 1.1 Examples from medium-term plans for the nursery and reception classes using formats based on areas of learning and footsteps (F) towards early learning goals (DFEE/QCA 2000a)

Area of learning: Knowledge and Understanding of the World – 2 EXPLORATION	January 2001
KEY LEARNING OBJECTIVES – knowledge, skills and understanding	SUPPORT ACTIVITIES
The children will be able to: • Explore objects. (F2) • Sort objects by one function. (F4) • Use a range of scientific vocabulary e.g. hard/soft. (F5) • Show an awareness of change. (F7) • Look closely at similarities, differences, patterns and change. (ELG)	• Explore sound: table top display of a collection of musical instruments and objects that make a sound • Investigate ways to make a small sound louder • Discuss this with the children. What did they do? • Investigate long and short sounds • Classroom display Peace at Last: children to draw/paint the sounds that kept Mr Bear awake
• Talk about what is seen and what is happening. (F4) • Begin to ask simple questions. (F4) • Ask related questions and record observations using pictures. (F7) • Ask 'why' and 'how' questions. (F8) • Talk about their observations using some scientific vocabulary in context. (F8) • Ask questions about why things happen and how things work. (ELG)	Storybooks to look at: Polar Bear, Polar Bear, What Do You Hear? What Can Pinky Hear? The Very Noisy Night Patrick Peace at Last – display 'Noisy' poems Further activities Making musical instruments

Table 1.2 Examples from medium-term planning matrix used by Key Stage 1 classes

MEDIUM-TERM PLANNER

Class: 3
Date: Spring 2001
Duration: 4 weeks

Subject: Design and technology
Topic: Books, stories and rhymes
Links to other
subjects: Maths, English, art, communication, number, problem-solving, independence

Learning intentions and levels	Activities/experiences	Assessment	Specific arrangements and resources
Use skills of measuring, cutting, designing to make cards with movement.	Look at examples of pop-up books with slides, pivots, and pop-ups. Where possible take them apart.	Planning and evaluation sheets.	*Rumble in the Jungle* Each child to make an example of each type of movement.
Use skills learnt to produce their own ideas.	Read *Rumble in the Jungle* and make moving animals e.g. elephant's trunk swinging, tiger's eyes opening, monkey swinging from tree to tree. Design a picture with a short story, for a young child, which has at least two moving parts.		Card, scissors, glue sticks, butterfly clips.

Notes (evaluation and amendments)

Table 1.3 How activities are grouped in the nursery and reception classes at Dalesview
First School and the learning promoted by the activities in
each area.

CONSTRUCTION

The children have a wide range of construction materials from which to choose.
Through their play, children explore and develop their understanding of the world.
They are encouraged to make plans and layouts and build models to enhance their play.
Their models are often used to promote further learning.

These activities help children to:

- 'persist for extended periods of time at an activity of their choosing'
- 'interact with others, negotiating plans and activities'
- 'talk activities through, reflecting on and modifying what they are doing'
- 'join construction pieces together to build and balance'
- 'construct with a purpose in mind, using a variety of resources'
- 'handle . . . construction materials safely and with increasing control'

IMAGINATIVE PLAY

Most children enjoy pretending to be a 'grown-up!' In our imaginative play area they
are encouraged to engage in role play and act out their own stories and ideas. We aim
to help children understand the roles and needs of others within a secure and relevant
environment. Children can find themselves in a hairdresser's, a supermarket, a hospital
or even on the moon!

These activities help children to:

- 'respond in a variety of ways to what they see, hear, smell, touch and feel'
- 'play cooperatively as part of a group to act out a narrative'
- 'show an interest in the lives of people familiar to them'
- 'use language to imagine and recreate roles and experiences'
- 'use language for an increasing range of purposes'
- 'initiate interactions with other people'
- 'engage in imaginative and role play based on first-hand experiences'

THE MARK-MAKING AREA

A wide range of mark-making resources is made available to all children. They freely
explore the marks they can make using pencils, crayons, felt-tips, chalks and pastels.
Children are encouraged to represent the world around them through their drawings,
and these are valued and shared by all. They also develop pencil skills through tracing
and pattern-making, and are supported in their attempts at letter formation.

These activities help children to:

- 'have a strong exploratory impulse'
- 'draw and paint, sometimes giving meaning to marks'
- 'engage in activities requiring hand–eye coordination'
- 'begin to use anti-clockwise movement and retrace vertical lines'
- 'begin to form recognizable letters'
- 'begin to use writing as a means of recording and communicating'
- 'use lines to enclose a space then begin to use these shapes to represent objects'

Table 1.3 (continued)

THE NUMBER AREA

Here we have an extensive range of equipment and resources to allow children to explore the areas of number, shape and space, size and dimension, pattern and logic. As in other areas, children are encouraged to make choices as to what equipment they need but they are supported and guided in its use.

These activities help children to:

- 'explore objects'
- 'talk about, recognize and recreate simple patterns'
- 'use developing mathematical ideas and methods to solve practical problems'
- 'show an interest in shape and space by playing with shapes or making arrangements with objects'
- 'show an interest in numbers and counting'
- 'show an interest in number problems'
- 'say and use number names in order in familiar contexts'
- 'count reliably'
- 'persist for extended periods of time at an activity of their choosing'

OUTDOOR PLAY

The outdoors presents children with a wealth of learning experiences. It is an opportunity to gain an awareness of space and the environment around them as well as exploring their own physical skills and coordination. Most importantly, it encourages children to play collaboratively and respect the needs and views of others.

These activities help children to:

- 'take risks and explore within the environment'
- 'be confident to try new activities'
- 'work as part of a group or class, taking turns and sharing fairly, understanding that there need to be agreed values and codes of behaviour for groups of people . . . to work together harmoniously'
- 'show care and concern for others, for living things and the environment'
- 'examine objects and living things to find out more about them'
- 'notice differences between features of the local environment'
- 'move in a range of ways'
- 'move with confidence, imagination and in safety'
- 'use a range of small and large equipment'
- 'recognize the changes that happen to their bodies when they are active'

PRACTICAL LIFE

Children are presented with a range of 'practical life' activities from which to choose. These reflect tasks they would experience in the 'real world', for example, threading, spooning, pouring, transferring, matching and polishing.

These activities help children to:

- 'have a high level of involvement . . .'
- 'persist for extended periods of time'

Table 1.3 (continued)

- 'be interested, excited and motivated to learn'
- 'select and use activities and resources independently'
- 'manipulate objects with increasing control'
- 'begin to try out a range of tools and techniques safely'
- 'engage in activities requiring hand–eye coordination'

THE READING AREA

We encourage children from a very young age to enjoy and value books and to see themselves as 'a reader'. A wide range of books is made available at every session with many opportunities to share them with a friend, an older child, an adult and parents at home. Very often, children memorize an early reader and feel proud to 'read' it to anyone who happens to pass!

These activities help children to:

- 'remember and talk about significant things that have happened to them'
- 'show an interest in illustrations and print in books and print in the environment'
- 'begin to be aware of the way stories are structured'
- 'have favourite books'
- 'enjoy an increasing range of books'
- 'begin to recognize some familiar words'
- 'recognize rhythm in spoken words'
- 'listen with enjoyment and respond to stories ... rhymes and poems and make up their own stories, songs, rhymes and poems'

SAND AND WATER PLAY

Sand and water provide children with opportunities to explore texture, temperature, capacity, floating and sinking, pumping, pouring, filling and emptying, and making patterns and pictures. Often, children use their imaginations to create shipwrecks or the lost world of the dinosaurs!

These activities help children to:

- 'talk about personal intentions, describing what they are trying to do'
- 'make comparisons'
- 'play cooperatively as part of a group'
- 'explore colour, texture, shape, form and space in 2 and 3 dimensions'
- 'notice and comment on patterns'
- 'use talk to organize, sequence and clarify thinking, ideas, feelings and events'
- 'use talk to connect ideas, explain what is happening and anticipate what might happen next'
- 'display high levels of involvement in activities'

Table 1.4 Mathematics in teachers' planning for the use of stories in their classrooms

Topic	Nursery	Reception	Year 1	Year 2
Predicting	Children encouraged to predict and retell.	Retelling of Three Bears story.	Select various items: e.g. apple, bread cheese, milk, wood, nail, paper, stone. Examine them. What will they be like in a week?	Questions related to Red Riding Hood: mental starter with number fans. If she left home at 9 o'clock and met the wolf half an hour later ...
Sequencing	Children encouraged to describe sequence of events.	Sequence of events in story both by telling and drawing pictures.		
Ordering	Dressing bear. Using washing line.	Use mathematical language of size. Order everyday objects.		
Number	Play 'Hickory Dickory Dock' counting game. Use 'stick on mice' to answer how many up to 12. Singing and retelling Ten in a Bed. Making models of mice to count.	Count every day objects prompted by items in Three Bears. Record numbers.	Dick Whittington: How many cubes can you wrap in a bundle? Story sums: children make up stories to fit number facts. Make up mathematical stories about characters in book.	

Table 1.4 (continued)

Topic	Nursery	Reception	Year 1	Year 2
Shape	Sort collection of round objects. Use curved shapes to make pictures and patterns. Bubble pictures.	Sort plastic bears of different sizes. Use Roamer to further develop understanding of number.	Snow White: reflections and symmetry. Give children 'half-pictures' and ask them to draw the reflection for the second half, using a mirror to help.	
Language		Understand full, half-full, holds more, holds less. Investigate ways of making small sound larger. Use language of time and be aware of time passing.		
Handling data				What big ears you have! Do bigger ears mean better hearing? Draw graph to show hearing distances. Use cupped hand on ears and compare results.

Introduction: setting the scene

Dalesview is a first school in a large and lively Yorkshire village surrounded by fields and fells. The school was built in 1973 and is semi-open-plan. When we arrived for our first meeting it was exciting to emerge from a long, dark, windy, and very wet drive over the moors into an entrance area glowing with children's art mingled with the work of mature artists. An image remains of delicious watercolours on heavy rag paper and aesthetically arranged collections of natural objects – and of welcoming teachers, at five o'clock still enthusiastic to talk about their school and our project for next term.

'Yes, we are blessed to work in a beautiful environment', Dawn Harrison, the head teacher, agreed with a colleague from college who was new to the school. 'But do not imagine it is a rural idyll! The children come from a variety of social backgrounds. Some live in the village in traditional stone cottages, many live in new developments of privately owned or council housing and a number live on quite isolated farms. Some parents work in rural occupations; others commute to one of the large towns thirty to forty miles away; others are unemployed.'

There are six classes at Dalesview. Lisa Williams teaches the nursery class in the afternoons. (She teaches a nursery class in another school each morning.) She shares a semi-open plan area with Alison Dowson, the reception class teacher. Gill Wilkins teaches Class 2 (Years 1 and 2) and Kate Peters teaches Class 3 (a mixed Year 2/3 class). Classes 4 and 5 do not fit into the age phase of our study. Dawn Harrison often works with groups in the central area between the classrooms. She has been head teacher at Dalesview for three years – a new experience after thirteen years in urban schools.

It seemed a good idea to begin our project in Dalesview for two reasons. Firstly, the school and college had for many years worked in a partnership to support the work of trainee teachers placed in the school. 'We feel we know you as friends as well as colleagues', Dawn said. 'That's why we have bravely agreed to try out this new book experience together!' Secondly, the nursery class was already an integral part of the school. Transition from nursery to reception class occurred within the same teaching area, and the social relationships between the children and the adults who worked with them were continuous. Nevertheless, when we had first talked to Dawn and her staff about our project they had been quick to say that, even in their cohesive situation, they had concerns about providing continuity of experience within different curriculum structures from the Foundation Stage areas of learning to Key Stage 1, where long-term plans are derived from the *National Literacy* and *Numeracy Frameworks* and Qualification and Curriculum Authority schemes of work. We agreed that exploring coherence and continuity in this relatively straightforward context, but where Years 1 and 2, and Years 2 and 3 are taught in mixed-age classes, would be a good way to find out how the project might develop in more complex settings.

The purpose of our first meeting was to explain to the teachers the overarching aims and rationale for our project, for them to identify specific questions they would like to investigate within it, and to clarify roles and responsibilities and a timescale for the case study.

OVERARCHING AIMS AND RATIONALE

The teachers had asked us to prepare a handout outlining what the project was about. (On rereading it, it sounds suspiciously like 'persuasive writing: advertisements, fliers and circulars, *National Literacy Framework* (1998), Year 4, Term 3!) Everyone endorsed the aims and rationale.

What is the aim of the project?
To provide examples of how children learn and how their learning can be supported, from the Foundation Stage areas of learning to the Key Stage 1 curriculum, through coherent and meaningful experiences.

Why is this important?
- The Foundation Stage takes place in a variety of settings; it is difficult to provide continuity.
- There is tension between the Foundation Stage guidance (areas of learning) and the National Curriculum (subject-based).
- It is important that our understanding of how children learn – in holistic ways, socially and emotionally as well as in their thinking, through experiences which stimulate their natural curiosity – lies at the heart of their early education and that it is not dominated by testing basic skills and league tables.

The teachers were keen to endorse the third point and to see how their school's values and philosophy, displayed alongside the photographs in the entrance hall, might be made explicit through the project. In what ways would it: promote teamwork; foster independence; value and extend children's capabilities and achievements in all aspects of their development; and provide a basis for lifelong learning?

Ambitious expectations indeed! We moved on to the next question:

What is the time scale for the book?

Spring 2001	Case study 1
Summer 2001	Case study 2
Autumn 2001	Case study 3
January 2002	The manuscript to be sent to the publishers
Spring 2002	Publication

The timescale was remarkably salutary. Yes, this was a practical and realistic project, which would be published. Yes, several members of the college team had written collaborative books before, working with colleagues in schools, and we thought we knew how to do it. 'How exciting!' one teacher said. 'Can we put children's work in it – and pictures?' We were in business.

QUESTIONS TEACHERS WANTED TO INVESTIGATE

As the discussion developed we established four key questions which all the Dalesview teachers agreed were central to their concerns:

- The nursery and reception teachers, Lisa Williams and Alison Dowson, plan for progression using footsteps toward early learning goals within areas of learning while the planning of the Class 1 and Class 2 teachers, Gill Wilkins and Kate Peters, is based on subjects and National Curriculum level descriptors. Is it possible to identify continuity in planning and progression in learning across these different frameworks, and can this be enhanced and made explicit?
- All the teachers make links between curriculum areas, underpinned by concerns for the holistic personal, social and emotional development of each child – but what level of curriculum integration is appropriate within a topic or theme and what kinds of links are best?
- How can we continue to use the *National Numeracy* and *Literacy Frameworks* and QCA and LEA schemes, but modify them significantly so they can be encompassed within a common theme and an integrated approach across the three-to-seven age phase?
- Can we, through this project, develop a model for developing continuity and coherence which can be used for different themes and topics, so that we avoid repetition but use our planning time economically?

This did seem a daunting range of rather broad questions. We agreed that neither the teachers nor the college tutors knew the answers. This would be a real partnership in exploration!

ROLES AND RESPONSIBILITIES

In order to find a manageable way of investigating these questions we drew up a planning schedule:

By 30 November
School agrees a theme to run through Foundation Stage to Year 2/3.

By 13 December
Tutors and teachers meet in school to decide how science, design and technology will be linked to language and mathematics strands, and to brainstorm possible activities within the theme.

By 12 January
Teachers agree to send medium-term plans for first half of spring term to college tutors.

15 January–15 February
Each tutor decides on a particular focus within their curriculum strand of the topic, and works with each age group for at least one session.

BOOKS, STORIES, AND RHYMES – AND CREAM CAKES

On 13 December – another dark, wet and windy evening – the college team met the teachers in school, over a cream cake tea. The teachers had decided on 'Books, Stories and Rhymes' as their theme. They felt that, although the focus was to be on exploration and investigation in science, design and technology, this theme also reflected the overarching importance of communication, language and literacy.

First it was necessary to decide how the four strands (science, design and technology, English and mathematics) were to be linked. Initially, links were too tight and artificial. We tried to identify a story or poem which could be linked to investigations in an aspect of science, then find ways of also developing technology, language and mathematics connected with the same story or poem: 'Jack and the Beanstalk' linked to science – growing beans in order to 'identify the features of living things' and 'look closely at change'; 'measure and compare growth in mathematics' – make pop-up bean plants in design and technology, and so on. The artificiality of trying to fit four subject areas into one story shoebox became clear as we tried to apply the same process to *The Very Hungry Caterpillar* (Carle 1998), 'See Saw Margery Daw', 'Jack and Jill'; and *The Lighthouse Keeper's Lunch* (Armitage 1994). But the discussion fired us up with ideas and the brainstorm was useful.

We finally agreed that each teacher would plan a five-week sequence of work in which stories and rhymes would be explored in different ways. Ongoing work in English and some in mathematics would be linked to a variety of stories. The tight links would be between specific stories and investigations in science or with planning, designing and making skills in design and technology.

Medium-term plans

By January the teachers had sent us their medium-term plans. All the staff use the North Yorkshire Curriculum Planning Disc as the format for their planning. The nursery and reception teachers used a format based on areas of learning and the early learning goals in the Foundation Stage guidance (Table 1.1). On each page a learning goal and the objectives leading towards it (referenced to the footsteps) are linked on the left. Learning objectives in blue are linked to ongoing activities in blue on the right-hand side of the page. Learning objectives in red are linked to activities in red on the right (also marked *) These are specific targets for this medium-term plan, which are teacher-directed. In these activities the teacher or another adult works with a small group.

In the nursery class, the medium-term plan for communication, language and literacy included as specific teacher-directed activities (in red) predicting and retelling a story (*), describing characters, settings and sequences*, making up a story using sequences of card window-frames depicting scenes and attaching speech bubbles*. Ongoing objectives, for play in a Nursery Rhyme Land role-play area, for example, were written in blue: interacting with others, negotiating plans and activities, turn-taking. Here the children were to help make the scenery, collect appropriate clothes, so that they could act out the rhymes, supported by a tape recording, sometimes with an adult playing alongside them to help develop storylines, vocabulary and discussion. In mathematics, plans included Hickory Dickory Dock games, (opportunities for technology here too?), counting up and down a number line using stick-on mice; games involving dice and dressing up the Three Bears in numbered articles of clothing. Science investigations would involve pendulums, clocks and timers, and in technology they would make clocks with flaps where the mice could hide.

In the reception class children would create a Jolly Postman role-play area, make card-and-stick moving characters to retell stories, do cross-curricular work based on the Three Bears, including instructions for making porridge. In science they would investigate sounds through all sorts of activities related to stories: *Peace at Last* (Murphy 1995), *Polar Bear, Polar Bear What Do You*

Hear? (Martin 1992), What Can Pinky Hear? (Cousins 1999), The Very Noisy Night (Hendry 1999), Patrick (Blake 1968) and 'noisy' poems. They would design and make musical instruments to create sounds linked to their favourite stories: Jack climbing the beanstalk, the giant's footsteps.

The planning matrix for Year 1 and Years 1/2 horizontally linked learning intentions, activities and experiences, assessment methods, and specific arrangements and resources for each subject, with key skills and links to other subjects identified at the top of the page (Table 1.2). In Year 1, stories would be linked to science investigations: Snow White investigated mirrors in a variety of ways, and the Princess investigated how many layers of different materials it would take to remove the discomfort of the pea – and various other objects that she found herself sleeping on. Sleeping Beauty could lead to systematic recorded enquiries into bedtimes, hours of sleep and the measurement of time in mathematics.

In Year 2, Little Red Riding Hood undertook numerous investigations into 'Grandma's' hearing. Are big ears an advantage? If not, what can make it easier to hear sounds; how, why? The Seven Dwarfs led to mathematical calculations of multiples of seven, and the measurement of precise differences between the heights of the Three Bears required related adjustments to the size and scale of their tables, chairs and beds. Books with pop-ups, slides and pivots were to be examined in order to create a pop-up book of Rumble in the Jungle (Andreae 1996), in which elephants swing their trunks, tigers' eyes open, and monkeys swing from trees.

Certainly, these teachers had planned for coherence across the curriculum, including areas not focused on in this case study: art, music, dance and physical and personal and social education. Progression was incorporated in the planning for each age group. How this would be demonstrated as a continuum across the three-to-seven age-phase would emerge in practice.

BIBLIOGRAPHY

Ahlberg, J. (1986) The Jolly Postman, London: Heinemann.
Andreae, G. (1996) Rumble in the Jungle (Big Book edition), London: Orchard
Armitage, R. (1994), The Lighthouse Keeper's Lunch, London: Scholastic.
Blake, Q. (1968) Patrick, London: Cape.
Carle, E. (1998) The Very Hungry Caterpillar, Harlow: Longman.
Cousins, L. (1999) What Can Pinky Hear?, London: Walker.
Hendry, D. (1999) The Very Noisy Night, London: Little Tiger.
Martin, B. (1992) Polar Bear, Polar Bear, What Do You Hear?, London: Hamish Hamilton.
Murphy, J. (1995) Peace at Last, London: Macmillan.

Chapter 2

Developing a scientific understanding of the world

Chris Sixsmith and Lisa Melbourne

Before starting a course in primary science, a number of first-year student primary teachers were asked about their understanding of the terms 'science' and 'scientist'. What words or phrases did they associate with these terms? The outcome was very interesting. Most of the students had spent at least twelve years in full-time education, and all were committed to becoming primary teachers. Despite this, the group identified the following words as those they most closely associated with 'science' and 'scientist':

> *Scientist*: older man, white hair, white coat, poor dress sense, absent-minded.

> *Science*: test tubes, difficult calculations, difficult theory, rockets, Bunsen burners.

When asked where these views had come from there was general agreement that they had come from the media – in particular films and television – and their own experience of science in secondary school. The stereotypes of science and scientists in films and advertisements had significantly influenced the views of these young people.

This conversation led to a consideration of the age at which these stereotypes begin to affect young children. Do they hold similar stereotypical views of science and scientists? Do they see science as remote and difficult? The work reported in this chapter is an exploration of the ways in which teachers encourage children to engage in scientific activity.

Some people would argue that the difficulty lies not with getting children to carry out scientific activities but rather with the way in which science is viewed. In the late 1960s David Bannister, drawing on the work of the American psychologist George Kelly, looked into the way children explored the world around them. He concluded that, in principle, children employed a scientific method. For Bannister, as for many others, the essence of science lies not in the carrying out of complex calculations nor the use of apparatus but rather in the process of creating and tesing hypotheses, coming to a conclusion and then using this knowledge to create new hypotheses. Bannister (1966: 362) explained George Kelly's theory:

> For Kelly, all men can be said to be 'scientists' in the sense that they have theories about their universe (not as systematic or sophisticated as the theories of professional scientists but theories nevertheless), and on the basis of these theories they have particular hypotheses (expectations) which are fulfilled or not fulfilled, and in the light of the outcomes of their 'experiments' their views are modified. Thus the model of man of Personal Construct Theory (George Kelly's theory of personality) is 'man the scientist'.

This general approach can be seen when observing children at play, particularly when they have a problem to solve. They will think of a solution and then try it out; if it doesn't work they will modify it and try that. They continue the modifying and testing process until they achieve the desired outcome. Take, for example Lynn, a three-year-old in a nursery class, who spent some time building a vehicle out of Duplo, part of which was motorized. When she showed this to her classmates and it failed to move, she began to realize that the motor would not carry the tall structure built on top of it. She immediately declared, 'This thing is too heavy,' and began to take off some of the Duplo pieces. She tried again to make her model move, still with little success. 'It needs more pieces off', she suggested, and proceeded to totally redesign her model leaving no bricks overhanging the motorized section. Her final attempt was successful, and her face lit up with pleasure. In many cases, once children have found a solution they will remember it, and when next faced with the same problem they will produce the correct solution first time. This indicates that children are active learners. They do not always simply absorb information by being 'taught' by others but also actively engage with the learning process. They construct their own understanding of the world by creating theories and testing them out, constantly modifying the theories to be consistent with their experience of the world. This view of the way children learn is totally consistent with the views of theorists such as Piaget, Vygotsky and Bruner (see pp. 107, 169–70, 171). Children are capable of acting in a scientific way without Bunsen burners and test tubes. Science is the process by which children find out about their world, not the equipment they use.

In the mid 1990s Rosemary Feasey suggested several areas of scientific activity that can be undertaken by young children. Among the skills needed are:

- *Basic skills*: To carry out investigations, for example using a magnifying glass, using a table to record results, using a ruler or other measuring instrument.
- *Observation skills*: To identify properties (such as roughness or smoothness), classify objects and form hypotheses about how things work.
- *Illustrations*: To record results.
- *Explorations*: To explore the properties of chosen objects.
- *Investigations*: To test out predictions while exploring or observing objects or systems. The children are involved in making decisions about how these tests should be constructed and carried out. It is when carrying out investigations that children will identify variables and create 'fair tests'. (Fair tests are tests in which the effects of one variable are investigated; all other possible variables are held constant to allow the effect of a single variable to be identified.) (Feasey 1994)

From this we can see that primary science is not concerned simply with 'doing experiments' using complex specialized equipment but rather with the development of skills, knowledge and understandings which allow children to explore the world around them. When you visit a primary classroom there is no evidence of white coats, Bunsen burners, test tubes. But the children are being taught science as part of Key Stage 1. In this chapter we provide some examples of how science is included in both the Foundation Stage and Key Stage 1.

Before moving on to consider these examples in detail it will be useful to consider some of the surrounding issues. *The National Curriculum for Key Stage 1* specifies nine *subject areas*, one of which is science. The Foundation Stage curriculum specifies six *areas of learning*: personal, social and emotional development; communication, language and literacy; mathematical development; knowledge and understanding of the world; physical development; and creative development

In the National Curriculum, science is recognized as a subject area in its own right. The Key Stage 1 teacher therefore has a range of clearly identified skills, knowledge and concepts which children are expected to learn. Since the Foundation Stage curriculum does not have an area designated as science, there is a great danger that teachers and others may attempt to identify a single area as pre-science, for example by deciding that 'knowledge and understanding of the world' is the 'science' element. Although this is tempting – and some links can be made in terms of the progression of skills and knowledge between the Foundation Stage and Key Stage 1 – care must be taken not to see the areas of learning in the Foundation Stage as simply a mix of Key Stage 1 subjects under different labels. To think of them as pre-science or pre-geography, for example, is to undervalue and undermine the Foundation Stage curriculum. It has been conceptualized and designed differently. This is significant when we are considering progression towards Key Stage 1.

Although the Foundation Stage does not identify science as an area of learning, it does have elements that relate to 'exploration' and 'investigation' in its key learning objectives:

- Explore by looking, feeling, touching, smelling and tasting and communicate discoveries.
- Enjoy finding out by exploration and investigation.
- Look closely at similarities, differences, patterns and change.
- Begin to ask questions.

The similarities between these key learning objectives and the areas of scientific activity suggested by Feasey are clear and help us to prepare the children for later work in science. The curriculum that is appropriate for the three-to-five-year-old does contain skills, knowledge and understandings that will form the basis of the child's study of science at Key Stage 1. It is not, however, a watered-down version of science. The activities suggested are driven by the nature and needs of the child, not by the future demands of the primary curriculum.

The nursery and reception classes at Dalesview School adopted the Foundation Stage curriculum and the 'early learning goals' in September 2000. The two teachers involved worked together to produce a coherent experience for the children. Both teachers wanted to make sure that the changes in the way the curriculum was organized and the subsequent impact on actual practice should be a positive experience for all involved. They wished to ensure that the best features of what was already in place were retained while looking to the possibility of creating an even more solid foundation for the children to build on. Towards this end both classes used a common planning format which linked closely with the 'early learning goals'.

At the same time, the physical organization of the curriculum in the Foundation Stage classroom is still heavily influenced by the beliefs and understandings of such Early Years visionaries as Maria Montessori, Frederick Froebel and the McMillan sisters (see pp. 2–4). There are ten activity areas: construction, sand and water play, imaginative play, practical life, mark-making area, outdoor play, creative area, reading area, number area, and 'small world' play. Each of the areas is linked to one or more of the six areas of learning. It is not possible or desirable to try and place science in only one or two of these areas as the learning that children carry out in each area will have an influence on their development of scientific thinking. In Table 1.3 the main elements of the work carried out in each of these areas has been outlined.

Even a brief consideration of these areas will indicate the integrated nature of children's learning at this stage. At any one time in the Foundation

Stage classes there would be some activities requiring supervision by a teacher or classroom assistant plus others the children were able to get on with under more general adult supervision. This means that in the nursery greater attention can be focused on the individual needs of the children than is possible with the higher pupil–teacher ratio in reception and Key Stage 1. At Dalesview this system is put to very good use by Lisa Willliams, the nursery class teacher, and Julie Barnes, the nursery nurse. Both are enthusiastic about, and dedicated to producing, high-quality education for the children in their care.

THE NURSERY CLASS: 'HICKORY DICKORY DOCK' (A PENDULUM)

The nursery children had been looking at the nursery rhyme 'Hickory Dickory Dock'. This had led to the setting up of two activities to do with pendulums, one which was supervised by an adult. The supervised activity produced a very interesting situation. The original activity had an inverted washing-up liquid bottle tied to a piece of string to make a pendulum. The bottle was filled with different coloured sand, and then as the pendulum moved and sand came out, a pattern was produced on the table under the pendulum. This worked reasonably well. The children observed the pendulum and the pattern and offered suggestions such as 'Try some of the black now.' Then, by chance, the pendulum broke and one child noticed that the pattern produced while the pendulum was broken was different from the original and commented on this. At this point the adult might well have passed over the remark and set up the pendulum as it was before; instead, she listened to what the child had said and followed that line, probing the children's understanding and extending the activity. Thus an unexpected and worthwhile learning experience was created when an adult recognized the opportunity. A significant amount of teaching that takes place in the Foundation Stage arises from situations such as the one just described, situations and opportunities that are difficult to plan for but when taken ensure quality teaching.

The second pendulum activity was designed to proceed without direct adult supervision. A pendulum was set up so that a weight could be swung to hit some skittles and knock them over. This activity was designed so that the children could not only observe the pendulum movements but could then use this knowledge to participate in a game: knocking over the skittles. It was interesting to see some of those who had been working on the supervised pendulum activity then move on to the second activity and immediately start to change the length of the string in order to alter the swing of the pendulum. Others could be observed trying to figure out how to hit the skittles, but not always to good effect. One small boy decided the way to get the pendulum to hit the skittles was to push the pendulum harder. This was a reasonable idea – but obviously one that would not work. He persisted for some time and was then stopped by another child, who came up and said, 'No. This is how you do it', and moved the skittles nearer. The children were able to explore their environment by observing, producing tentative predictions and then trying out their solutions.

THE RECEPTION CLASS: SOUND STORIES

In Alison Dowson's reception class, the children had made up their own story about Miss Harrison, the head teacher. The head was trying to find somewhere quiet to work but was disturbed by a range of different noises in different parts of the school. This had been the basis of work on sound. Having created the story, the children were engaged in a number of activities, two of which related to it. As with the nursery, one activity was closely supervised and the second was under more general supervision. The supervised activity required the children to go around the school tape-recording examples of the sounds featured in their story and thereby creating a 'sound story'. The children were clearly highly motivated and keen to get on with the task. Again, the integrated nature of the Foundation Stage curriculum is apparent with the use of ICT to explore the area of sound.

The second activity required the children to explore the sounds different instruments made. They carried out this activity with enthusiasm and arrived at some simple conclusions. Alison Dowson prepared them for the activity by asking a series of questions: 'What do you have to do to make the sound?', 'Has anybody found something that you shake?', 'What is Joanna doing to make the sound?' When Alison left the group the children continued to explore the instruments and then began to sing 'Jingle Bells'. Others arrived at the table and were helped in the task by those already there. They then went off to complete a worksheet. Towards the end of the session the tape-recorder group came back to the classroom and the children gathered to listen to the story accompanied by the tape.

YEAR 1/2: CLASSIFYING, HYPOTHESES, RECORDING: (THE PRINCESS AND THE PEA AND OTHER TALES)

Mrs Gill Wilkins, the Year 1 class teacher, adopted a slightly different approach. Rather than getting the children to work on worksheets outside the classroom, this class all did science at the same time. Gill, a very experienced class teacher and master storyteller, began her lesson by reading the traditional fairy story of the Princess and the Pea. To be able to listen to a talented storyteller weaving a web of enchantment for a group of six- and seven-year-old children was a delight. The children were rapt, hearing a story they had no doubt heard before but still transfixed by the retelling. When the story was finished and they had been given the opportunity to raise questions and make comments, the next phase of the lesson was explained.

The children were going to be carrying out a series of activities relating to the story. In each of the activities they were to explore an element of science. For two of the activities teams of three children were given the job of setting up the activity and helping the rest of the class to carry out the activity and then record the results. Although the activities were designed and resourced by the class teacher, the children 'running' the activity clearly felt some ownership of 'their' task and involved themselves in discussions as how best to organize the activity for maximum effectiveness.

The activity most directly related to the story required the children to try and work out what objects were hidden inside six different 'feely bags'. They did this through touch, identifying key features of the object and then attempting to match these with objects they knew. In some ways this could be seen as developing the skills required for classifying objects, clearly a skill that the children would have to further develop in their later studies of science. The team who gave clues as to what it was most appropriate to focus on helped them in this. This produced some interesting language The team then recorded the results in a table. Again, this was an activity that develops a key skill in studying science.

The second activity required the children to locate a pea through a number of thicknesses of cloth. This replicated the pea and mattresses of the fairy story. The team helping with this task reduced the number of thicknesses of cloth until the child carrying out the task was able to detect the presence of the pea. Again, the team recorded the results.

In addition to these activities the children were involved in two other scientific explorations related to stories they had covered earlier in the term. The first of these came from the work they had been doing about the story of Dick Whittington. The children were given equal-sized squares of different types of fabric (for example cloth, hessian, wool). They were then asked to estimate the number of cubes they could wrap up in each of the squares. Having made their estimate, they had to carry out the task to see how many they could actually wrap up and then record this. The children were later encouraged to look for patterns in their results to see if there was any link between the results and the nature of the different types of cloth. Those working on this task were clearly surprised, not necessarily by the fact that different materials should be capable of holding different numbers of cubes but by the size of the difference. This finding was further emphasized by the teacher's enthusiasm and encouragement. She took the results and then, by skilful questioning, led the children first to explore why the differences might have arisen and then to start to produce their own hypotheses capable, needless to say, of leading to further exploration and investigation.

The story of Snow White and the Seven Dwarfs gave rise to the fourth activity. The children had made a collection of mirrors and other objects with reflective surfaces: kitchen foil and shiny spoons, for example. This had led to activities relating to mirrors. The pupils were asked to make a shape out of plasticine or multilink, break it in half and then see if they could use the mirror to make it appear whole again. Alternatively there were a number of half-pictures which the children could make appear whole by using the mirror at the correct angle. The activities with the mirror gave rise to a great deal of interest and excitement as the children made genuine discoveries about the use of lines of symmetry. 'This is a really funny teddy bear', 'Hey, Tim, Tim, this has got four legs–look!' The children engaged in the initial activity and then further explored the situations, discovering aspects of mirrors they had simply not been aware of before.

YEAR 2/3: CINDERELLA (THE PROPERTIES OF MATERIALS AND FAIR TESTING)

Kate Peters's class had been listening to the story of Cinderella, the well-known traditional fairy tale which, by its very nature, engaged the children's interest. The teacher had decided to make use of their interest to encourage them to explore the properties of materials. The National Curriculum for Key Stage 1 clearly identifies areas the children should study in relation to materials, one being 'properties of materials'. The teacher focused on the part of the story relating to the clock striking twelve and set up an activity in which the children had to use three hammers made of different materials to hit a piece of either wood, plastic or metal. They then had to make a judgement as to which material created the loudest noise and which the quietest before being asked to explain their results and say why they thought what they had done was a fair test. The children were organized into three different ability groups and each child was given a worksheet with instructions and a place to record their results. They were encouraged to work in pairs and to help each other.

This was an interesting activity because it came somewhere between an exploration and an investigation. The children were being asked to carry out an exploration, but were also being asked to think about the dimension of fair testing related to investigations. All the children managed to complete the task with varying amounts of assistance from their peers or from the adult working with them. The results were interesting. All the children had to write their answers to the questions, and this did raise an additional difficulty for those less able at writing who might well have produced shorter and less well-considered answers because of this difficulty which might well have contributed to an apparent difficulty with science. This is a dilemma that teachers face in all areas of the curriculum. They have to constantly make judgements about the effect that ability in one aspect of the curriculum may have on a child's ability to express his or her knowledge and understanding in another area. The problem shows itself perhaps most clearly in written tests such as the SATS (Standardized Assessment Tasks), where a child's difficulty with English may well influence judgements about his or her knowledge and understanding of mathematics.

When asked why they thought the material they had chosen was best suited to the purpose of making a chime, the answers fell into three categories. One group of children simply said that it was best because it made the loudest noise. A second group said it was best because it was wood, attributing the loudness to the material rather than attempting to identify the relevant property of the material. A final group attempted to explain the property of the material that was relevant. Some said, 'It was hard', others, 'The wood did not move'.

When asked about the fair test, there was again a range of answers. Some of the children had only a simplistic understanding of the idea of fair testing and gave answers such as 'We banged it hard'; most of them had some idea that fair testing required the control of variables. Almost without exception they focused on one variable such as 'We hit them the same', or 'I hit them in the same place' or 'I hit them as hard as each other'. These children are beginning to understand the concept of fair testing but are still bound by the immediate context and focus on one variable. Within this age group there was clear evidence of qualitative differences in the children's scientific thinking.

We have described what happened during one week in Foundation Stage and Key Stage 1 – but what of the progression? Has the introduction of the Foundation Stage, with its different way of conceptualizing the curriculum, made progression more difficult? Looking at the work carried out in the four classes, is there clear evidence of progression? The overall theme for the period of the case study was 'Stories, books and rhymes'. This did not seem to be an obvious starting point for science, but it is clear that in the two Key Stage 1 classes science was being taught. In the Foundation classes, the skills and knowledge that would provide a firm foundation for further work in science were also clearly present. It would not be possible to track every aspect of the work through all four years, but here are some examples which illustrate this progression.

The development of the scientific activity of 'exploration' can be seen throughout all four years. In the Foundation Stage classes exploration is synonymous with the idea of play as the most relevant and effective way in which to engage young children in learning. Exploration comes easily to them in a supported and exciting environment. Therefore a pendulum corner set up in the nursery was an invitation for them to explore and re-evaluate their early scientific thinking and knowledge. In reception, the children were given opportunities to explore sound through adult-led activities, but also, as in the nursery, resources were offered and questions posed for children to further explore that initial activity. Early in Key Stage 1, the 'exploration' is more finely tuned. Children are moving away from playful exploration to more clearly focused activities designed by the teacher. Exploration – the 'doing', the 'trying out' – remains, but the focus is now moving towards a systematic engagement by recording results. By the end of Key Stage 1 the exploration element has become integrated into a more investigative approach. Children not only explore and record, but also raise issues about, for example, 'fair-testing' and possible explanations of their results.

From this it seems clear that although the Foundation Stage curriculum does not have an area of learning specifically referred to as science, it does have the potential to give children the foundation skills, knowledge and understandings that can be further developed in Key Stages 1 and 2. The skill of the teacher remains central to the effective teaching of young children.

FOLLOW UP IDEAS

Take an area of ongoing provision: for example sand play, water play, large construction toys or role play. Think about how these resources are presented to each of the four year groups. What opportunities for scientific under-standing are available, and how do these progress from nursery to Year 2?

If, for instance, we choose water play:

- What concepts or skills could be developed through these resources?
- What additional apparatus might be given to children in each class to help scaffold their learning?
- How would you assess the learning which has taken place?

BIBLIOGRAPHY

Bannister, D. (1966) 'A new theory of personality' in B.M. Foss (ed.), New Horizons in Psychology 1, Harmondsworth: Penguin.

Feasey, R. (1994) 'Scientific investigations' in R. Cherrington (ed.), The ASE Primary Teacher's Handbook, London: ASE/Stanley Thornes.

Goldsworthy A. and Feasey, R. (1994) 'Making sense of primary science investigations' in R. Cherrington (ed.), The ASE Primary Teachers Handbook, London: ASE/Stanley Thornes.

Chapter 3

Design and technology: the danger of cutting corners

Owain Evans

It was clear from the Dalesview design and technology planning documents that they were based on the principle that there should be no barriers between the Foundation Stage and Key Stage 1 classes and that it is both possible and desirable to maintain a spiral curriculum throughout the children's education from nursery to Year 3. This principle informed decisions not only on 'what the children will learn' but also 'how they will learn'. The quality and sophistication of the work completed by the pupils are indicative of the benefits of such a seamless transition where continuity and progression are a priority. It is a far cry from another school, where it was said that 'the only difference between the design and technology outcomes at reception and Year 6 is that there are fewer fingerprints on the older children's pop-up Easter chick cards'. At Dalesview the expectations are high, the staff are committed to providing a well-balanced and complete experience, and the pupils are keen and motivated. They do enjoy the advantage of occupying a semi-open-plan site, with the nursery class next door to the reception class.

WHY DOES DESIGN AND TECHNOLOGY MATTER?

Why should Dalesview place so much effort and emphasis upon a subject that in some schools is still seen at worst as a messy nuisance or at best as a Friday afternoon fill-in? What does design and technology offer that merits such attention? The subject may sound like a rather new and strange area of study for younger children. Yet to some extent it builds on traditions established for a hundred years. Though these long traditions do not fully prepare one for what is included in the subject today, the expectation is far more than just an amalgamation of this historical parentage, which includes woodwork, cookery, dressmaking and so forth. It is this significant shift in emphasis that has led parts of the teaching profession and the wider community to have a somewhat clouded view of it: 'What is this beast? Is it art, science or craft?' It is also unfortunate that the name of this National Curriculum subject has become muddied: we already had 'information and communication technology', and in the last (1999) revision of the National Curriculum what had been 'art' became 'art and design'. Apart from ICT, design and technology differs from all the other subjects taught in schools today in that it does not possess a direct lineage such as those enjoyed by mathematics or music. These subjects can rely upon all educators having direct, first-hand experience and understanding of the nature and feel of the subject. Libraries are full of maths textbooks, colleges have known genera- tions of music graduates, yet there is no substantial body of academic development or international research background in the field of design and technology. Indeed, few of today's practising teachers will have studied it while at school, particularly when very young. ICT, which began its nation- wide development relatively recently, with the 1981 introduction of one computer per school, has since enjoyed vastly greater support and funding from government and industry than has ever been bestowed upon design and technology. Yet those familiar with the potential of a comprehensive design and technology curriculum maintain that the immediate and long- term benefits are as great and far-reaching as those for ICT. What is the evidence for this claim?

> It is an active study . . . it involves the purposeful pursuit of a task to some form of resolution that results in improvement (for someone) in the made world. It is a study that is essentially procedural (that is deploying processes/activities in pursuit of a task) and that uses know- ledge and skills as a resource for action rather than regarding them as ends in themselves. The underlying drive behind the activity is one of improving some aspects of the made world, which starts when we see an opportunity to intervene and create something new or something better.
>
> (Kimbell *et al.* 1991)

In a school context, children will use knowledge and skills for a particu- lar purpose or as part of the processes involved in making changes to their material well-being as and when these are needed. This will be on a 'need to do basis' rather than that of acquiring knowledge for its own sake or performing a skill in isolation, such as carving a mitre joint or baking a Victoria sponge simply to display mastery of a particular aspect of wood- working or cookery. A distinct and essential characteristic of this new subject, design and technology, is that it provides pupils of any age or ability with opportunities to develop their capability through combining their designing and making skills with knowledge and understanding from all areas of their learning in order to create high-quality solutions. This is a distinc- tive process and combines intellectual and practical skills in a manner in which thought and action reciprocate. The interaction of mind and hand, reflection and action, is a powerful tool in developing the child's creative ability: from hazy impressions, to imaging and modelling in the head, through trialling, to prototype solutions.

Clearly this is a demanding process, and so it should be if high-quality solutions are expected; however, there are particular aspects that need to be considered when working with very young children, especially if they have little prior experience of such challenges. Whatever the children's age, the challenge presented to them must be relevant and motivating, located within a context they are familiar with and that they understand. They will then appreciate when a successful outcome has been generated. If the challenge is beyond their experience then they will be forced to rely upon an adult to make evaluations and judgements about the suitability of their proposed solutions.

MOVING PICTURES

The children at Dalesview were making moving pictures employing some of the paper-engineering mechanisms they had previously investigated and linking their designs to the theme of nursery rhymes and folk tales. They had investigated how moving pictures operate, where the folding elements are hinged, how the sliding pieces move and what effect is achieved by having one part of a design held by a paper fastener that allows it to rotate. They knew what it was that made such a picture interesting, amusing and satisfying; so, in turn, they could and did judge their own efforts with some authority. They had thought about the designs and had begun to appreciate the nature and complexity of the planning required to produce these sophisticated children's books. They were becoming aware of the sequence of construction and assembly. The various rhymes and tales were studied in order to explore their potential for employing this technology.

The manner in which the children are to tackle the challenge needs to be considered carefully and will depend largely upon the extent of their prior experience. For instance, it would be unrealistic and unproductive if all pupils were expected to produce 'working drawings' prior to beginning any making (although some children are remarkably adept at producing visual evidence of their ideas and should be given the opportunity to do so). The place and purpose of drawing within the overall process of generating designs needs careful consideration and requires its own developmental programme. Ron Ritchie (1998) has written a valuable book on this subject. Initially it may well be more productive to focus upon developing children's oral communication skills so as to help them explore the challenge with their peers and speculate with them about possible solutions. Indeed the opportunities in design and technology sessions for meaningful collaborative dialogue – for example the use of complex sentences, specific vocabulary and general instructions – arising from exacting activities are often cited by Early Years teachers as a most valuable attribute of design and technology sessions.

The nursery class: the mouse ran up the clock

In Lisa Williams's nursery class children worked together to make a grandfather clock in such a way that a mouse could run up and down it. The clock case had an opening door which permitted the mouse to be seen inside. The mouse was attached by a paper fastener to a card disc placed behind a slot which ran the length of the case. As they recited the nursery rhyme 'Hickory Dickory Dock' the children took it in turns to move the mouse. They all clapped when the clock struck – plenty of multi-sensory experiences here as well as the pleasure of collaborative achievement.

The reception class: the giant, the caterplllar and the wolf with ferocious jaws

In the reception class, Alison Dowson's children worked individually at first. They each designed a nursery rhyme character with body parts which were to be attached by paper fasteners so that they could move. Their original small drawings had been enlarged on the photocopier so that they would each fill an A4 card. The children cut out these big designs using appropriate scissors. I particularly remember Joanne's elongated giant, Mark's ferocious wolf with an opening jaw and Jonathon's rather brave attempt at making a hungry caterpillar. Enlarging pictures in this way was a clever move on Alison's part as it made cutting out the designs a more manageable task while not detracting from their original ideas. The uniform-sized puppets could then be fixed into a collaborative class big book using self-adhesive Velcro pads.

Class 2: the sun, the moon and animals that talk

Gill Wilkins' Year 1/2 class used different pop-up mechanisms, including rotating circles (as used to make a moon move across the sky) and a 'V' fold (for example, the speaking animal). Gill was demonstrating to one group how to use a circle cutter to produce a very precise curved slot, whilst another adult helped a boy named Peter to fold card accurately. They combined these techniques in different ways to create sequences of scenes in a collection of pop-up storybooks, each child having decided on a particular scene from a tale chosen by a small group. The skill base available to the children facilitated some really ingenious and satisfying results.

Class 3: moving stories

The Year 2/3 children made individual storybooks of traditional folk tales or recently published stories. Each child was asked to employ two or more mechanisms from the range he or she had previously learned to make, including sliding pictures, floating layers and pivoted arms. The pupils were supported by their process diaries which detailed the stages through which the initial designs were developed into sophisticated products. The complexity and quality were impressive. Susan, for instance, was justifiably proud of her Jolly Postman.

DESIGN AND TECHNOLOGY AND LANGUAGE DEVELOPMENT

Several strategies were used consistently throughout the design and technology sessions at Dalesview First School that contributed to the overall success of their programmes. The emphasis placed upon real dialogue – adult to child and peer to peer – was clear. Due time was given for extended and well-focused explanation and discussion. The children were encouraged to engage in the dialogue, and special care and sensitivity were employed to encourage the reticent newcomer. Without losing the management of the class the teachers expected the pupils to voice their ideas and opinions. This policy began in the nursery, where the sense of a negotiated environment was evident; the teacher requested her class to consider a plan proposed by one of the children to make the mouse run up the clock. The children were asked if they would like an adult to help them with a specific task such as moving the clock, a construction that was now quite large. In the top class, the teacher asked if anyone had thought of a way of solving a paper engineering problem encountered by one pupil in the previous session: how to make a neat hole in the centre of a large piece of card. Although direct commands by the adults were used when necessary, particularly to emphasize safe practice, on the whole the teacher was not a dominant voice. In turn the children were expected to keep their talk at a reasonable level while they were working. This policy ensured that the teachers could monitor the class's progress and that the children were able to attract help when needed.

Despite the dreadful weather that battered the windows, the classes operated without undue noise and valuable discussions were held:

Adult to nursery child: How are you going to make this end square again, Jenny?

Child: I'll do this … then this [a neat one-finger push] … and it comes out … a box!

Nursery child to adult:	I want a hole . . . here . . . the hole maker won't fit.
Adult:	You're right . . . it's not long enough, is it? Let me use my sharp pencil, very carefully. And please may I give your nose a wipe?
Reception child to adult:	The arms should be . . . on to here . . . but I don't know where to make the slot so they move up and down. [He was trying to establish the fulcrum point].
Adult:	If I mark that spot with a pencil then you can try using a drawing pin and then move the arm until it does the right action.
Child:	Yes thank you . . . then I can cut it.

After Gill Wilkins, the teacher, had directed the Year 1/2 children at the start of their session, a child approached her and asked, 'Do we have any scissors that cut with a wavy pattern? . . . I tried with straight ones but it wasn't neat enough.' In Kate Peters's Year 2/3 class a child was trying to use a circle cutter. However, the paper was swivelling around: 'Please, Sam, will you hold the paper? . . . There . . . I'll be very careful.' These older children were making quite complex moving picture designs to illustrate big books of folk tales. Each page had to include two or three types of movement. The combination of mechanisms required very thorough forward planning and high standards of measuring and cutting, none of which could have been expected unless the essential prior work had been covered and the under-lying philosophy set in place.

PERSONAL, SOCIAL AND EMOTIONAL DEVELOPMENT

At no time when I was at the school did I come across that most dispiriting sight: a queue of children waiting for their class teacher to perform some simple task for them. This may be sharpening pencils, rubbing out mistakes, using 'the sharp scissors' or, worse still, seeking permission to go off and manage a task that the teacher knows they are quite capable of performing safely for themselves. A common feature of the classroom that operates in that inefficient way is the unwillingness or inability of the teacher to develop in their pupils appropriate and essential attitudes, aspirations and skills, or to provide an environment which facilitates and promotes such independence. The successful classroom will characteristically be one where the pupils are engaged and motivated by their prescribed assignments, are aware of their scope for independent activity; where they are capable of working cooperatively and the resources are accessible and clearly identified. These attributes should form a common strand in the spiral curriculum that children deserve to experience throughout their schooling. Although these personal qualities and attitudes are not stated as explicit goals in the National Curriculum they are clearly identified in the *Curriculum Guidance for the Foundation Stage* (DFEE 2000). For instance:

Personal, social and emotional development

- Learning to respect themselves and others;
- Learning about relationships;
- Developing a positive disposition to learn;
- Having opportunities for problem solving.

Physical development

- A safe, well-planned and resourced learning environment;
- Building on the children's developing skills to promote confidence and independence.

Creative development

- Feeling secure to try new experiences and ways of doing things.

For these characteristics to become an expectation there need to be whole-school policies in place which promote and reinforce them. Through such policies the real working ethos of the classrooms will be established by the responsible adults so that the way they promote these expectations is of the utmost importance. If the adults do not value peer support or differing opinions then their pupils will soon lose interest and comply with these limiting habits. If on the other hand the adults respect their pupils and expect them to become motivated learners there are certain essential skills that will greatly assist in that outcome.

Of all those essential skills that, once mastered, liberate the child and, in turn, the responsible adult, the effective and appropriate use of scissors must be amongst the most significant. Why so important? It is not just that it avoids the unnecessary queues and the child's dependence upon the adult's assistance. In cutting a piece of material a child is making an irreversible public statement which indicates that an act has been performed; it demands both technical manipulative ability and self-confidence. The child is called upon to make a judgement about the characteristics of the required tool necessary to manage the task and about the place and scale of the act. The success and quality of the resulting work reflect directly the expertise of the operator. This expertise is the result of structured and sequential experiences that take young children from novice through to expert. Through a group of carefully graded exercises in a series of environments involving the use of different sizes and types of scissors and various kinds of paper and card, the universal skill can be developed. Children then become liberated learners by acquiring the ability to take decisive actions in an appropriate way and so are no longer dependent upon another's intervention. This epitomizes the aims of the Foundation Stage. Yet all too often scissors skills are assumed to be in the child's repertoire, unlike, say, the ability to use a hand drill. (A teacher would expect to have to teach that.) A child may enter school being able to manipulate a pair of first scissors to chop through a piece of paper held by an adult, but that is not a true indicator of an acquired universal skill. It may be assumed that once the child is able to manage that first assessed activity then all further development can be left to chance and good fortune. This is surely a recipe for disappointment. The very familiarity of scissors as a tool may lead us to neglect the need for progression of skill development and continuity of experience.

One can identify a series of experiences with scissors that are necessary for a child to acquire true independent competence. For some pupils these experiences may take place at home before they start school, whereas others will need these exercises later in their career especially if they suffer from some impairment or delayed development. Children who have had multiple transfers between schools may appear in the top junior class with minimal apparent ability and will then require discreet, sympathetic support if they are to cope with activities already easily managed by their new classmates. The list below is not a complete list of scissors skills, and they are not necessarily in an appropriate sequence. A similar list should be identified for a sensible extension to include the proper use of pliers, wire strippers, snips, craft knives and circle cutters:

- Watching scissors being used in the correct manner;
- Appreciating that once a cut has been made then the article can be reshaped or divided;
- Using plastic scissors to cut clay or play dough;
- Using 'safe scissors' (usually round-ended) to cut into thick paper, possibly with an adult manoeuvring the paper;
- Using safe scissors to cut along straight lines on various papers/cards;
- Using safe scissors to cut along wavy lines on various papers/cards, an activity that can be repeated with increasingly sophisticated shapes and higher expectations of accuracy and quality;
- Using special scissors (such as zig-zag or frilly edge) to manage the above;
- Using pointed-ended scissors when necessary;
- Using pinking shears to cut fabric and appreciating the need to care for such equipment;
- Using utility snips to cut hard plastic or thick card;
- Using appropriate scissors to cut difficult materials such as crepe paper, cooking foil or stretch fabric.

Certain specific techniques will need to be taught, such as cutting a shape from the middle of a piece of material or using two different types of scissors for one task. At any stage some children may be helped by having one handle of the scissors clamped to a desk so that they have only to think about moving one blade. Two-handed models are also available, enabling an adult to assist the novice when appropriate. Whatever scissors are available, they must be capable of providing a neat cut; poor-quality tools will make any task frustrating and the acquisition of the skill more problematic. The old adage remains very true: 'The scissors must cut and the glue must stick.'

One must always keep in mind those children who are left-handed and those uncertain about their handedness. This concerns not just the availability of the correct type of scissors but the very way in which the cutting activity is presented. Many adults who work with children will have learnt how to demonstrate the 'left-handed approach' to any task. The learning scenario can be quite complex when parents are left-handed but the child is by nature right-handed, or where the two parents exhibit both preferences and the child has acquired a mixed impression. It is very common to find left-handed children who, having learnt to arrange their fingers so that they can cope with right-handed scissors, when presented with the correct design find they can no longer manage. The combination of fine motor skills, level of hand-to-eye coordination and self-confidence required for this everyday task is very demanding and complex. It deserves attention and requires a concerted programme throughout the child's schooling.

Ben, in Alison Dowson's class, was left-handed and new to the school. Initially he tried to model the way other (right-handed) children were using their scissors. Alison had decided that the best way to help Ben was to stand behind him, guiding his left hand and supporting the paper. She encouraged him to 'be different' and not to worry because he used his left hand.

DEVELOPING DESIGN CAPABILITY

Writing in 1993, Tina Jarvis maintains: 'At present primary school children have limited opportunities for learning to identify needs for themselves, as many teachers usually decide what the children will do or make.' (6) A few years later, a Year 1 teacher proudly showed me a wall display of twenty-six articulated toads whose legs were connected to their tongues. They were identical. The pre-printed shapes had been cut out by the classroom assistant; the children had merely collected the required pieces and fastened them together. 'We didn't have time to waste on more than one lesson – and anyway they are not good at cutting.' (6) This moving-picture exercise was the sum total of the design and technology for the year. Jarvis continues:

In the past teachers have tended to protect children by providing only the materials they need and detailed instructions so that they are guaranteed a good end product, but this will restrict their opportunities to learn to chose appropriate tools and materials and so solve further problems as they arise.

(1993: 7)

The situation has generally improved during the intervening years, especially the level of making skills, although there remains concern in many quarters about the quality and extent of the children's ability to design (Ive 1999). Sadly there are some places where both the requirements of the National Curriculum – and the rights of the children – are still being neglected, as witnessed at an infants school where the head teacher said: 'Of course our children are too young to use glue and scissors.' Children are quite capable of mastering these intellectual, aesthetic and manual skills given the right environment and the support of adults who see the purpose and value of exploring this challenging subject.

The very youngest children in the nursery class at Dalesview were encouraged to be aware of the design potential of what could have been a teacher-dominated activity. The reception pupils were able to create their own designs for moving pictures, using the appropriate sharp tools, under careful supervision. By Year 1 they were able to use such tools with confidence and safely. The aesthetic delight of the Year 2 children was obvious from the effort and consideration they expended on ensuring that all the lettering was tidy and attractive and that the finished products were a complete success. The school is providing a series of experiences for its pupils which will encourage them to become 'autonomous and creative problem-solvers'.

Design and Technology prepares pupils to participate in tomorrow's rapidly changing technologies. They learn to think and intervene creatively to improve the quality of life. The subject calls for pupils to become autonomous and creative problem-solvers, as individuals and as members of a team. They must look for needs, wants and opportunities and respond to them by developing a range of ideas and making products and systems. They combine practical skills with an understanding of aesthetics, social and environmental issues, function and industrial practices. As they do so they reflect on and evaluate present and past design and technology, its uses and effects.

(DFEE/QCA 1999: 90)

SUGGESTED IDEAS

Track a design and technology skill through your school:

- Where is it introduced?
- Where is it employed?
- Where is it assessed?
- Where is any remedial help offered?

Scissors use is an obvious choice. However, you may wish to examine a skill that is introduced at a specific point within your school, such as sawing or sewing.

SUGGESTED FURTHER READING

Christine Bold's book (1999) looks specifically at the complex issues of continuity and progression and offers some useful photocopiable activities to help with staff development and pupil assessment.

Ron Ritchie's book (1998) explores children's learning through design and technology. It identifies how the specific disciplines of the subject run in parallel with strategies employed when teaching it – identifying needs, generating and developing ideas, planning, implementing and evaluating.

BIBLIOGRAPHY

Bold, C. (1999) *Progression in Primary Design and Technology*, London: David Fulton.
Ive, M. (1999) Unpublished report to the annual conference of the Design and Technology Association (DATA), Coventry.
Jarvis, T. (1993) *Teaching Design and Technology in the Primary School*, London: Routledge.
Kimbell, R., Stable, K., Wheeler, T., Wozniack, A. and Kelly, V. (1991) *The Assessment of Performance in Design and Technology*, London: APU/SEAC.
Ritchie, R. (1998) *Primary Design and Technology: A Process for Learning*, London: David Fulton.

Chapter 4

Traditional stories and rhymes: 'Goldilocks, don't you do owt!'

Katharine Langley-Hamel

Literacy is linked to children's self-esteem. This influences ways in which children perceive themselves as learners throughout their lives. If young children are to learn effectively and to become confident communicators and enthusiastic readers and writers, they need opportunities to develop skills within a lively and relevant context. We should start from what children can do, building on their strengths.

I was interested in the ways in which schools develop a theme across ages, introducing new skills and understanding while consolidating what children already know. This was demonstrated by the way in which Dalesview School approached the subject of traditional rhymes and stories from the nursery class to Year 2. Planning addressed children's changing needs and set greater challenges.

The importance of traditional stories, songs and rhymes highlighted in the *Curriculum Guidance for the Foundation Stage* (QCQ/DFEE 2000) is developed in more detail in the National Literacy Strategy for Key Stage 1 (DFEE 1998). What relevance have these traditional forms for today's children? What can they learn from them?

Stories help us make sense of our own lives. Children tell stories about their own experiences every day, as they find it easy to think in narrative. Traditional stories provide opportunities for children to become aware of the language of story, to join in repetitive phrases, to play with language and to recognize familiar patterns. These stories reflect a range of cultures and allow children to increase their knowledge and understanding of the world by moving from the familiar to the unfamiliar. Much of children's early language relates to their actions in the present. Retelling stories and reflecting on settings helps them to think in more abstract ways and draw on different types of vocabulary. Traditional stories have a distinctive type of language and structure. This helps children to retell, re-enact, rewrite or recreate their own versions of these stories.

I was delighted that the children and teachers of Dalesview First School shared my enthusiasm for traditional stories and were planning to use them as a focus during the first half of the spring term. I wanted to see how children responded to these texts and how they saw themselves as story-tellers and writers. The nursery and reception classes were planning a topic on stories, books and rhymes to address the six areas of learning which form the basis of the guidance for the Foundation Stage. The children were to be given the opportunity to:

- Listen to favourite stories and nursery rhymes, joining in with repeated refrains anticipating key events and important phrases;
- Describe main story settings, events and principal characters;
- Pay attention and take account of each other's views.

Lisa Williams, the nursery teacher, had created a lively and colourful environment to support the development of each aspect of literacy. This included opportunities for children to share books, stories, songs and rhymes and to engage in role play. (The role-play area reflected the nursery rhyme theme.) In addition, Lisa encouraged children to retell aspects of stories using props.

WHAT DID THE CHILDREN DO?

I introduced myself to a group of four children from the nursery who were enthusiastically retelling stories and rhymes. I wondered to what extent they supported one another as they each told stories and rhymes. Would they collaborate or compete? What sort of detail did they add? Would they make links between the stories and rhymes and their own lives by adding details drawn from their own lives and experiences? The following examples of their retelling of stories and rhymes gave me clues. Nathan and Tracey, for example, were working together to ensure an accurate retelling of 'the Humpty story':

Nathan: I'll do you the Humpty story,
            Humpty Dumpty sat on a wall,
            Humpty Dumpty had a great fall,
            All the King's men
            Couldn't put Humpty together again.
Tracey: No, you mean horses, you have to do the horses.
Nathan: I know, I'm just doing them.

It was also clear that the children collaborated well in their retelling of Goldilocks and the Three Bears. Here they also brought their own experiences to the story, building on each other's responses. (Note how Tracey decides the bears will have soup!) Their experiences of parental reprimands and their own experiences of saying sorry are also woven into the narrative.

Nathan: I know the one about the girl who goes in the cottage, but she doesn't tell her mummy. She heard a voice in the woods and it came from the house and she just went in.

Tracey: Yes, she went in and on the table she saw the food, it was soup.

Nathan: It wasn't soup, it wasn't, it was porridge and she ate it all up.

Leanne: And it was too salt and then it was all right.

Nathan: And the baby bear didn't have none left.

Tracey: No, none left.

Nathan: And the bears comed up and they said, 'Look, it's Goldilocks!' And then Goldilocks runned away.

Leanne: The bears roared like this: 'ROAR'! And Goldilocks was frightened.

Tracey: The bears were horrible to Goldilocks, but she shouldn't eat up other people's porridge. She ran home and her mummy said, 'Goldilocks, don't do owt again', and she said she was sorry.

Nathan: But she wasn't really sorry at all.

The children demonstrated clearly that they understood listeners to the story required detail in order for their interest to be engaged and maintained. Such details came from their own experience and were introduced as a result of their willingness to adapt the story.

Alison Dowson, the reception class teacher, planned to develop the children's experiences and awareness of stories and rhyme further. She encouraged the children to discuss them, and to develop their confidence and enjoyment in answering and asking questions about them. Starting points were familiar stories and rhymes, and a range of role-play activities. Alison demonstrated how a traditional story can help children to move from the familiar to the unfamiliar while retaining a simple structure. Nursery rhyme characters are introduced into the context of the story about an enormous watermelon, a variant of the well-known story *The Great Big Enormous Turnip* by Leo Tolstoy.

Alison shared a big-book version of *The Enormous Watermelon* with the children, providing an enthusiastic first reading, and modelling skills of reading with intonation by using different voices for different characters. During a second reading she drew their attention to the dialogue, presented in a different colour in the printed text. She encouraged the children to recap on the structure of the story, join in with certain parts of the text and to predict the next character to become involved.

Then Alison introduced a range of props to support role play. An article of clothing or an object was used to represent each nursery rhyme character. Several children took part in this. Some chose props to represent different characters, giving reasons for their decisions, while others volunteered to take part in the role play. The rest of the class discussed the sequence of events in the story and organized a running order. The children then

Figure 1.1 Reception class children's drawings of nursery rhyme characters

performed a choral reading of the story. They read with expression, supported by the coloured text and picture cues.

A range of appropriate group activities reinforced the learning which had taken place. Some children worked on the characters within the story, recapping on their role in that story or nursery rhyme, drawing pictures with simple captions. Others were engaged in word-level work, using words from the text as a starting point. Figure 1.1 shows how one group of children in the reception class matched drawings of nursery rhyme characters to their names. Another group engaged in further role play. They were given the freedom to re-enact and explore aspects of the story independently with the support of the resources used in the previous session.

The children extended their knowledge of the language, structure and vocabulary of story, making intertextual links, weaving characters from one setting into another. They were able to discuss characters, plot, setting and motive and participated in group discussions, putting forward their own ideas and listening to the ideas of others.

Gill Wilkins, who teaches Year 1/2, extended the work on traditional stories to include fables. She began by reviewing the children's knowledge of traditional stories. They considered patterned and predictable language and the organizational features of fable. They developed their knowledge of character through dialogue. She asked the children what they understood by a traditional story, and they offered a range of responses, including the following:

Joss: They were written a long time ago.
Ellie: We don't know who wrote them.
Paul: They can get changed.
Jake: They start 'Once upon a time' and they finish 'happily ever after'. They all have to do that.

Gill asked the children to name some traditional stories. Responses included Sleeping Beauty, Puss in Boots and the Elves and the Shoemaker. She asked them if they knew any traditional stories from other cultures. They retold the story of *Jamil's Clever Cat* (French 1999), linking it to 'Dick Whittington' and identifying similarities and differences.

She then introduced work on the fable, asking children to define a fable. Responses included:

Joe: They tell you about a lesson – they all have to do that.
Thomas: They tell you about the boy who cried wolf. In King Frog they tell you that frogs should have been good and not grumpy.

Gill introduced one of Aesop's Fables which was unfamiliar to the children, the Fox and the Stork. The story was introduced as a sequence of pictures. The children were asked to consider what dialogue might have taken place between the characters. This was recorded in speech bubbles whilst the teacher explained the need to record speech in a special way. Gill focused on the time connectives, which are important in retelling the events of a story in order. These included 'then', 'later', 'next', 'finally', words that help listeners and readers make sense of the story. Gill wrote the time connectives on the whiteboard so that children could use them later when retelling the story of fox and the stork. Gill used a familiar teaching strategy, circle time, to encourage them to retell the story collaboratively. The children listened to the initial retelling of the story and suggested possible exchanges between the fox and the stork. They gave reasons for their choices based on their interpretations of the characters.

In addition, they considered the feelings of the characters and linked these to their own experiences. During a whole-group retelling of the story during circle time, each child listened to the previous speaker, adding his or her own contribution. The use of time connectives helped them to structure the retelling of the story.

Kate Peters teaches Class 3 (Year 2/3 children). Here traditional stories were to be explored to consolidate the children's previous knowledge, extend their experience and develop their skills in reading and writing. The class was to be introduced to a mixture of traditional stories told in their original form, and retold from characters' different perspectives, and with alternative endings. Considerable emphasis was placed on discussion, as the children were encouraged to reinterpret stories. During the single session related below, the teacher capitalized on earlier work in reading and discussion. She encouraged the children to put what they had learned to good use in their own writing. Kate talked to the children about the ways in which stories could be changed, discussing the need for some elements to remain the same to maintain a clear structure. She invited the children to suggest alternative endings.

While working on their own versions of traditional story endings, children talked to me about what they were doing. I was interested to see that some of them were able to demonstrate in their writing the abilities the nursery children had shown in adapting oral story to reflect their own experiences and interpretations.

Cinderella

Steven: The boy was poor to begin with, and Cinderella had some beautiful dresses. She found the Prince and got married. The stepmother's going to die.

Laura: Cinderella doesn't get married to the Prince. She's going to be the servant. She's going to stay poor. She might get a bit of money for being a servant, but then it's going to end, not happily ever after, just the end.

Goldilocks

Ben: Goldilocks is going to be nice and not frightened. She's going to see the porridge and think, 'Now, shall I eat that or not?' But she doesn't eat it because the bears might find out. That changes all the story.

WHAT CHILDREN SAID ABOUT WRITING STORIES

Children talked about their experiences as authors, and were able to identify aspects of story writing which were easy and the complexities they faced. They told me that they found the simple retelling of traditional stories easy because of their familiarity with the structures, characters and language. A variety of ideas were expressed about the need to plan stories before writing them. Some children saw this as very helpful:

Scott: You might forget it otherwise, when you're busy writing.
Sarah: You need to think before you start, but just try to keep it in your head.

Some children found it hard to move away from the familiar story ending. Some stories had action-packed but rather abrupt endings!

Richard: I will eat you for my dina said the wolf he got his hamer and noct it down then got the pigs then ate the pigs up this is the end.

The children told me about the sort of language they needed to use in writing in the style of a traditional story: 'once upon a time'; 'one day'; 'happily ever after'; 'beautiful'.

As I was talking to the children it became obvious that many of them were able to incorporate their knowledge of the genre of traditional stories into their writing. As with the younger children, they made links with their own experiences, and this was reflected in their written storytelling. Some children, like Ben, were still not ready to move away from the familiar version in writing their stories (Figure 1.2), while Donna wrote a vivid and detailed reinterpretation of Snow White (Figure 1.3). Her description of the feast at the palace has all the hallmarks of a six-year-old's birthday party.

Snow White said I am so happy lets have a party. Thay had ice crem and crisps and choclate buns and a big cake and cochlott fingers and ciking legs cheese on crakas and they all lived happily ever after.

Children realized that traditional stories may be altered. Those who succeeded best recognized the need to plan their alterations in advance and to choose their language carefully to reflect the appropriate style.

The strength of whole-school planning lies in the way it reflects and respects children's current stage of development and understanding while providing clear links with the next stage of development in which they develop the abstract skills of retelling and recreating stories in writing. As has been demonstrated, traditional stories and rhymes provided a rich learning context for children across all the age phases in the infant school. At each level, the children were able to build on their existing knowledge to extend their experiences, and to move confidently from the familiar to the unfamiliar. Success resulted from a series of carefully planned, relevant and enjoyable activities.

The ε pigs and the big bad
Woln. Thay bilt a house out
of the Wood then thay bilt
a howes of bricks then
the wolf came then he
bowe let me in no no we
will not let you in
I will eta you for my ding
I will eta you up for my dina
He got his Hamer and
nock t it bown then got
the pigs and ate the pigs
up the end .

Figure 1.2 Ben, in Year 2, was not yet able to reinterpret the story of the Three Little Pigs

FOLLOW-UP IDEAS

Tape-record versions of stories children retell

Traditional stories come from the oral tradition; they were passed on by being retold. It is important that children are aware that we value the ability to tell as well as write stories. Encouraging them to tape stories shows them that we value and can keep a permanent record of their versions of stories. It allows them to retell stories without the pressures associated with writing, and to compose more confidently at greater length. They are happy to add detail which may have been left out of written versions. Above all, it provides an opportunity for success.

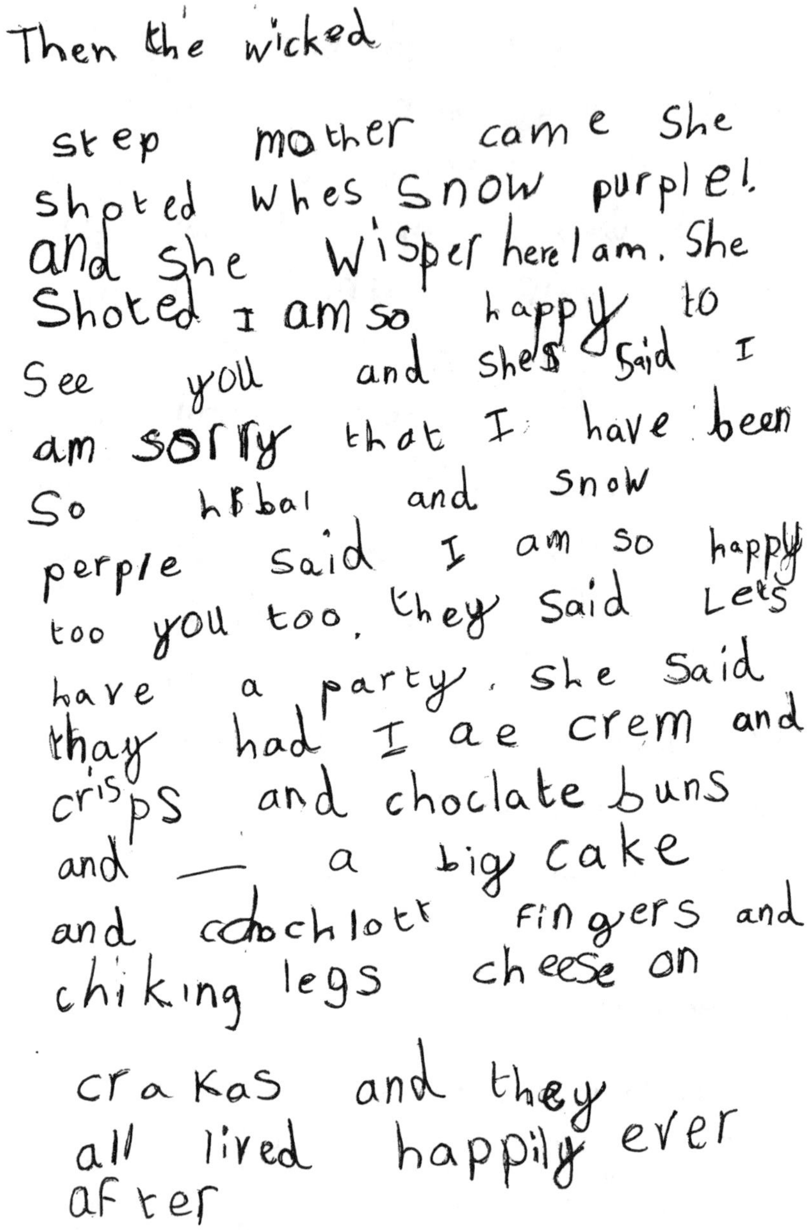

Then the wicked

step mother came She
shoted whes Snow purplel.
and she wisper here l am. She
Shoted I am so happy to
See you and she's said I
am sorry that I have been
So hßbal and Snow
perple Said I am so happy
too you too, they Said Lets
have a party, she Said
thay had I ae crem and
crisps and choclate buns
and ___ a big cake
and cochlott Fingers and
chiking legs cheese on

cra Kas and they
all lived happily ever
after

Figure 1.3 Donna's vivid and detailed reinterpretation of the story of Snow White

Tape-record character interviews

Children can explore the feelings of different characters by recording interviews in which characters are given the opportunity to explain their actions or to discuss their feelings about events in the story. This process can become increasingly sophisticated and can help the children to understand different perspectives.

Role play

Transform the role-play area into a setting for a traditional story. This can support children's learning in a variety of ways:

- It can develop vocabulary in a meaningful context;
- It can support children when acting out aspects of the story;
- It can encourage them to link their own experiences with the story;
- It can develop awareness of the motives and feelings of characters in the story.

Use art to develop an understanding and enjoyment of story

The connections between retelling and drawing a story are clear. Children can engage in a range of creative activities which bring stories to life and develop an understanding of story structure, plot and character. The 'moving characters' the children designed and made to retell stories – described in Chapter 3 – are a good example.

SUGGESTIONS FOR FURTHER READING

Dewsbury, A. (1999) *How to Assess, Plan and Teach Fiction and Poetry (1) First Steps*, Oxford: GHPD.
   A clear overview of stages of development which are linked to a comprehensive range of strategies for teaching fiction and poetry to young children.
Goodwin, D. and Perkins, M. *Teaching Language in the Early Years*, London: David Fulton.
   This informative and readable book describes and promotes good practice in Early Years education.

BIBLIOGRAPHY

French, F. (1999) *Jamil's Clever Cat: A Bengali Folk Tale*, London: Frances Lincoln.
Tolstoy, A. (1998) *The Great Big Enormous Turnip*, London: Little Mammoth.

Chapter 5

Sum stories: developing children's mathematical knowledge with meaning

Margaret Foster and Robin Foster

> Stories are also commonly used to start up play in role-play areas. The story will provide the structure for the play but children can amend the plot and characters to reflect their own priorities and interests.
>
> (Dowling 2000: 142)

The use of stories in the primary classroom is a very powerful way of teaching many aspects of the curriculum. Nutbrown (1994) notes that 'stories are a vital means of extending children's thinking and fostering their knowledge and attitudes'. The mathematics lesson is no exception as many stories lend themselves to being used to allow mathematical thinking to be developed or displayed. Hughes *et al.* (2000) make a strong case for encouraging children to tell stories in a mathematical context in order to give a real-world focus to the mathematics they are doing. Hurst and Joseph (1998) indicate that stories can be seen as *teachers* for the children. The linking of the hearing of stories to specific prompts to action or play is emphasized by Marion Dowling (2000).

With the introduction of the National Numeracy Strategy it might be felt that some of the wider uses of story in a very open-ended way might not be suitable, possible or attainable as there is so much work to be completed in the daily mathematics lesson. A strong emphasis on number and focused objectives might be thought of as not being achieved by the apparent imprecision of the use of stories in a haphazard kind of way.

In Dalesview First School, the teachers felt that story provided the children with the enthusiasm to explore mathematical ideas. They had also used story successfully as an element in whole-school planning, explaining that it allowed them to explore topics in ways that involved a range of subjects and all of the children. The supporting material for the National Numeracy Strategy and previous good practice, particularly at Foundation Stage and Key Stage 1, makes it important to include aspects of story in the daily mathematics lesson. We were interested in finding out how teachers integrated story and storytelling into the teaching of the National Numeracy Strategy.

We had discussions with the Dalesview teachers about their use of stories, talked to them about their plans, observed them in their classrooms and looked at the children's work. Two specific aspects of story were selected for investigation with the Foundation Stage and Key Stage 1 children and their teachers, and these resolve into two main areas. The first asks the more traditional question which relates to the explicit use of storybooks in the classroom: How are references to books read by the children or to them by the teacher exploited in the daily mathematics lesson? This includes references to the way the practitioners relate their work in the mental and oral starter to real life, using and applying aspects of their thinking; additionally, in the main part of the lesson when they record mathematics based on the story with which they are familiar.

The second area tends to be more tentative and exploits the children's use of stories they create from situations they are presented with. This connects more closely with the area of problem-solving, which involves looking at the children's use of storying to make sense of a situation to which they bring an understanding.

During the course of the work teachers had focused on the children's reactions to stories. They had explored how their pupils used mathematical language in their explanations of their mental working and how these related to the stories that inspired the questions. The children's recording was also investigated.

The numeracy consultant for the school was particularly keen that the National Numeracy Strategy should be fully implemented. In their planning the teachers paid particular attention to carrying out these requirements fully and explicitly. Their planning included full references to medium-term plans which covered the topics of the Numeracy Strategy, and their additional preparation made continual reference to mathematics and the opportunities for relating mathematical topics to the stories they were using in the classroom (see Table 1.4). The teachers were questioned about the specific ways in which they planned for the use of story and their ideas are indicated below.

THE NURSERY CLASS

In the nursery class, Lisa Williams used traditional stories and rhymes such as 'Ten in a Bed'; the rhymes were used to reinforce counting forward and back. They also used their play activities to make stories. Through cooperative play the children talked about the farm, zoo and traffic activities set up in the classroom. Then Julie Barnes, the nursery nurse, played a game of skittles with the children. She highlighted the mathematical language by using numbers orally and showing written numbers accompanied by counters to represent the number of skittles knocked down.

THE RECEPTION CLASS

The reception teacher, Alison Dowson, chose stories which were considered especially appropriate in the mathematical context. They included:

> The Three Bears
> *Kipper's Toy Box*
> *Ruff*
> *Nine Ducks Nine*
> Cinderella
> *Five Little Ducks*
> Counting rhymes/action rhymes

Alison Dowson also used the circle time to develop story and mathematics. She used the story of *Kipper's Toy Box* and selected a toy frog to pass around the circle, asking the children to count forwards and backwards. In the main section of the daily mathematics lesson activities were designed to link the stories to mathematics.

YEAR 1

The medium-term plans for Year 1 (extra to Numeracy Strategy) included the following:

Topic: Books, stories and rhymes

Learning intentions and levels	Activities/ experiences	Assessment	Specific arrangements and resources
To support and enhance work done in the oral and mental parts of the numeracy hour.	'Story sums': children make up stories to fit number facts. Make up mathematical stories about characters in books.	Response and recording.	Spend a session recording these stories. Prepare a book.

The Year 1/2 teacher, Gill Wilkins, approached the topic through English. She chose traditional stories and rhymes including:

The Elves and the Shoemaker
The Old Woman who Lived in a Vinegar Bottle
Puss in Boots
Aesop's Fables
Little Red Riding Hood

The children were encouraged to make up simple stories based on the traditional ones. Encouraging them to talk about numbers and size in the stories drew out aspects of mathematical language.

YEAR 2

In Year 2 the teacher, Kate Peters, composed 'real-life' mathematical problems to accompany stories read in English. In the oral and mental starter children were asked questions and similar ones were provided on a worksheet for the main part of the lesson.

Topic: Books, stories and rhymes

Learning intentions and levels	Activities/ experiences	Assessment	Specific arrangements and resources
Use mental addition or subtraction or simple multiplication and own strategies to solve story problems about number in 'real life'. Mental, mental with jottings . . . Explain orally/ write a number sentence to show how it was solved.	Various questions linked with books, stories and rhymes – mentally with answers on number fans/worksheet with written questions: Little Red Riding Hood left her house at nine o'clock. She met the wolf half an hour later. 'What time did she meet the wolf?' 'Snow White': 'how many knives and forks needed for seven dwarfs?' Mummy Bear was 75 cm tall; Daddy Bear 20 cm taller. 'How tall was Daddy Bear?'	Mental starter with number fans.	Whole-class worksheets. Children suggest own stories.

DISPLAY AND ROLE-PLAY AREAS

Another major feature of the teachers' planning was the way it included provision for role play. In each of the classrooms role-play areas were devoted to the theme of stories. The children were encouraged to play in the environments created and explore their own learning by role-playing aspects of the stories. The planning also included display, which allowed children's own work to be displayed as well as material chosen by the teacher to illustrate aspects of the story.

CONCLUSION

The staff at Dalesview were able to integrate the work on story with the National Numeracy Strategy. Their delivery of the daily mathematics lesson was in accordance with the advice given by the local authority's numeracy consultant. At the same time the work on story fitted quite naturally into their planning. The extra planning relating to the use of story supported and extended the work from the daily mathematics lesson. This mix of features combined to give the children a rich experience of mathematics. The experience was enhanced by the teachers' skill at directing at the children clear questions devised to develop their language and curiosity.

FOLLOW-UP IDEAS: GROUP ACTIVITY

Work in a group of three or so people.

One of the group members should retell, in their own words, the story of Goldilocks and the Three Bears. Discuss your responses to these questions, and others you think useful:

- Do the children agree with the story?
- Were any repeated phrases used when telling the story?
- How did the storyteller keep the hearers' attention?
- If you were telling or retelling this story to Key Stage 1 children, how would you arrange it?
- What, if any, are the mathematical aspects of the language or story you might wish to highlight?

SUGGESTED READING

Dowling, M. (2000) *Young Children's Personal, Social and Emotional Development*, London: Paul Chapman.
See Chapter 9, which deals with mathematics.

BIBLIOGRAPHY

Aubrey, C., David, T., Godfrey, R. and Thompson, L. (2000) *Early Childhood Educational Research*, London: RoutledgeFalmer.

Dowling, M. (2000) *Young Children's Personal, Social and Emotional Development*, London: Paul Chapman.

French, V. (2001) *Five Little Ducks*, London: Walker Books.

Hayes, S. (1999) *Nine Ducks Nine*, London: Walker Books.

Hissey, J. (1996) *Ruff*, London: Red Fox.

Hughes, M., Desforges, C. and Mitchell, C. (2000) *Numeracy and Beyond*, Milton Keynes: Open University Press.

Hurst, V. and Joseph, J. (1998) *Supporting Early Learning: The Way Forward*, Milton Keynes: Open University Press.

Inkpen, M. (1993) *Kipper's Toybox*, London: Hodder and Stoughton.

Nutbrown, C. (1994) *Threads of Thinking: Young Children Learning and the Role of Early Education*, London: Paul Chapman.

Dalesview: a happy ending?

By the time the chapter writers had completed, discussed and revised their drafts and the editors had collated them, it was November 2001: nearly a year since the Dalesview teachers had identified the four questions they hoped the 'Stories, books and rhymes' project might explore. Hilary Cooper and Chris Sixsmith carried out a quick analysis before they sent the case study to Dawn Harrison and her staff for their comments. Chris attended a staff meeting in January for a final review of the project.

CONTINUITY IN PLANNING AND PROGRESSION IN CHILDREN'S LEARNING

Despite the different curriculum planning frameworks used in the Foundation Stage and at Key Stage 1 a clear progression could be traced through each strand of the project. In science, children moved from exploration based on asking questions arising through play, which adults helped them to explore further, to investigations which became more sustained. Gradually they learned to record results systematically. By Year 2 they were using concepts of fair testing to interpret their findings.

In design and technology, a progression in skills and in the level of sophistication displayed in interactions between children and adults was seen to be promoting an increase in independence. The moving characters the children designed and made to act out their stories became increasingly complex constructions. When we consider language development, the nursery children demonstrated their ability to retell rhymes; they were able to relate the rhymes to their own experiences; moreover, they corrected and supported each other. In the reception class the children were able to tell their own versions of well-known stories; they gradually extended their understanding of dialogue and character. By Year 2 many of the children were able to write their own versions of traditional stories that were, in some cases, quite detailed. The teachers traced a progression from reception to

Year 3 in each area of mathematics, through problems they posed in the context of traditional stories.

Maybe this is not surprising. Children inevitably mature and develop increasingly complex skills, irrespective of curriculum structure and to some extent irrespective of the skilled interventions of adults; indeed planning for progression is an integral part of both the Early Years and National Curricula. Yet it was reassuring to find that our project provided slivers of clear and focused evidence of this as a seamless process across the two stages.

WHAT LEVEL OF CURRICULUM INTEGRATION IS APPROPRIATE WITHIN A TOPIC?

At the planning stage we had rejected a straitjacket of artificial links. Nevertheless science, design and technology and mathematics seemed to benefit from a basis in story, not just because this seems to an adult mind to create coherence and a reason for doing 'this' rather than 'that' but also because, as Katherine Langley-Hamel's chapter on developing literacy through story made clear, children engage with stories and are motivated by them: stories are familiar, safe, part of the rich wholeness of experience.

There were aesthetic dimensions to the topic too. Science in the nursery class arose from children's observations and questions about a sand 'pendulum' set up initially to create patterns. Aesthetic decisions were an integral part of the success of the moving pictures created in design and technology.

THE NATIONAL NUMERACY AND NATIONAL LITERACY STRATEGIES

There were, of course, opportunities for relating traditional stories to the objectives of the National Literacy Strategy, although these were not restricted to the literacy hour. The teachers taught mathematics through the numeracy hour, but they identified and exploited many opportunities within the numeracy framework to link problem-solving in mathematics to stories, both within the numeracy hour and at other times.

HAVE WE FOUND A MODEL FOR PLANNING FOR CONTINUITY AND COHERENCE?

Having mixed-age classes increases the complexity involved in ensuring that there is clear progression and continuity for all the children. Planning at

Dalesview is based on a two-year cycle, designed to ensure that children make good progress but do not repeat topics. Such an approach requires teamwork and careful subject coordination. It has to be carefully monitored, and at Dalesview there is a programme to monitor and evaluate both planning and practice at regular intervals. Teachers welcome support and guidance with their planning and value feedback from lesson observations. The staff view the fact that the school is partly open-plan with shared areas as a positive benefit in that teachers are aware of the activities going on with other classes. They also feel that the system of class assemblies in which children share the work they are doing with the rest of the school helps to make all staff better aware of what is happening all through the school.

Another very important element that underpins continuity is that in addition to drawing on QCA documents, the North Yorkshire Planning Disc, the National Curriculum and the guidance for the Foundation Stage, the staff also strive to develop 'key skills' in every curriculum area. These are:

- communication;
- the application of number;
- information technology;
- problem-solving;
- working with others;
- improving own learning and performance.

This, coupled with the ability of staff to recognize and respond to the individual learning needs of the children, has led to an effective way of planning for continuity across the Key Stages.

SCHOOL VALUES AND PHILOSOPHY

Dalesview colleagues had wondered how the results of the project might reflect the values of the school. The staff believe the school should be:

- A caring place where everyone feels secure, valued and quality relationships are important;
- A positive place for developing and celebrating high standards;
- A successful place where individuals work hard to fulfil their own potential;
- A place where fairness, honesty, trust and a sense of belonging are promoted.

In short, could we identify within the project opportunities for teamwork and also experiences which foster independence, which value all children's capabilities, and form a basis for lifelong learning? We tracked back for some illustrative examples. In science, at different times, children worked in supportive pairs, in different leadership roles within the whole-class context and in spontaneous and flexible collaborative groups. In design and technology, there were many examples of the importance of dialogue both between children and adults and between children. All the story-focused activities were collaborative, giving the children opportunities to correct each other with humour and respect, to offer suggestions about other points of view and ways of doing things, to re-enact stories together through play. In each of these contexts they were learning to take each other's feelings into account.

Across all these activities the children were learning to respect themselves and each other; they were finding out about relationships. At the same time they were learning to develop positive attitudes to learning and to solving problems. The success of the school lies in no small part in the approach and attitudes of the staff. These are, perhaps, best summed up by Gill Wilkins.

> In our school the teachers have a social and professional commitment to the children and to each other. This is the 'mortar' which holds together the bricks of the curriculum. We are fortunate in that we all genuinely respect and like each other so working as a team comes naturally. The semi open-plan design of the school enhances this sense of unity.
>
> The world, at the start of the third millennium, is a vast and potentially bewildering place for a young child. Even to an adult it seems there is no end to the pursuit of knowledge. All the more reason therefore that children's education should have cohesion and continuity, leading to the security in which children flourish.

Part 2

Clappersgate Primary School and Brantwood Nursery School: Africa – music, art and drama

Table 2.1 Nursery medium-term plan showing focus for each week

Nursery: first half, summer term	
Week	Focus

1   *Familiar meals at home*

Breakfast (cereal), lunch (sandwich), tea (fish fingers, potatoes, carrots)
    prepared by children; hygiene; equipment
Favourite meals – pictures for bar chart
Growing food – carrot and parsnip tips, cress, beans, fruit pips
    Measure growth

2   *Places to eat*: picnics, fish and chip shop

McDonald's role-play area – roles of staff and customers – menus, ordering,
    assembling, eating, costs, paying
Food from other countries/cultures – parental involvement – Spanish,
    Oriental, Italian, African

3   *Africa*

Walking Through the Jungle}   stories   –   African images
Handa's Surprise (Brown 1997)}   –   animals
                                                 –   climate
                                                 –   ways of life
African music – rhythms
Role-play area (mud walls, straw roof, drums, pictures, African clothes,
    textiles)
Fruits from Africa – oranges, pineapples, mangoes, passion fruit, bananas,
    guava – comparing, tasting – senses

4   *Art*

African textiles – colours, patterns
Hot colours
Colour mixing (paint)
Prints
Weaving – in fur, leather, feathers, wool

Replica clothes from Africa in children's sizes
    Ayabah
    Sarong wrap
    African fez
    African head-tie
    African printed headscarf
    Wrap-around skirt
    African shorts

Table 2.2 Table showing how weekly focuses in the nursery were linked to areas of learning (DFEE/QCA 2000a)

Nursery: first half summer term

Mathematics	*Communication, language and literacy*

Food/fruits   –   size, shape
Seeds/stones –   weight
                     –   patterns
                     –   comparisons
Ingredients/weight
   when cooking
Mixing/blending ingredients,
   consistencies
Portions – sharing foods
Favourite foods – graph
Growth of seeds, etc.
   –   comparisons
   –   non-standard units
	Descriptive language – feeling,
	   smelling, tasting
	Variety of foods/fruits and
	   associated language
	Appropriate language – slicing,
	   peeling – cooking food – boiling,
	   grilling
	Books/print – fiction – food
	   stories – Africa
	Non-fiction – menus, recipes,
	   price list, images of other
	   cultures – Africa
	Role play – McDonalds

Physical	*Personal and social*

Manipulative skills
   – using tools to prepare   **FOOD**
   and eat
Healthy diets – foods that
   are good for us
Gross motor skills – 'Bean' game
Senses – tasting, smelling, touching
   seeing, hearing – foods
	Helping prepare food/meals
	   – turn taking, sharing,
	   co-operating
	Enjoyment from sharing food/
	   meals
	Increase awareness of people's
	   differing needs, preferences,
	   cultures
	Caring for growing seeds

Knowledge and understanding	*Creative*

Observing, preparing and tasting
   foods/fruits
Changes during cooking
Equipment used to prepare and
   cook food
Reasons for variety of food eaten
Increase awareness of foods
   from other cultures
Africa   –   food/fruits}
            –   animals}   *Handa's*
            –   climate}   *Surprise*
            –   lifestyle}
Use of IT to create patterns
Growing foods
Sources of foods
	Patterns, shapes and textures of
	   foods raw/cooked
	Aromas of foods/playdough
	Colours of foods
	Colour mixing – purples/hot
	   colours – using dough, food
	   colouring, paints
	
	African colours (hot) – textiles
	   patterns – use of *Handa's*
	   Surprise
	Creating patterns in IT
	Observational drawings/paintings
	   of foods
	Role play – McDonalds

Table 2.3 Reception class teachers' lesson plans for the 'Africa' theme

Focus	Concept/skills	Activities	Resources	Assessment Knowledge & understanding of the world
1 Introduction Story Handa's Surprise (Browne 1997) Identify people, culture, climate, landscape and food (FRUIT)	Developing an awareness of the world beyond our local environment recognizing cultural similarities/differences, landscape, food (fruit),	Locate Kenya on a map/the globe. (AFRICA). Brainstorm what we know ... Has anyone had a holiday there ...? Collect artefacts?	The Big Book of Handa's Surprise. Globe, world map, information books	Check children's knowledge – where do I live? (Refer back to 'Kendal' topic) Can they locate England ... Africa?
2	animals, homes, climate (effects of) hot and dry; monsoon. Savannah, grassland, desert, jungle. Fruits – observe, describe, compare, classify (use of the senses). Extension of vocabulary size comparisons.	Begin ABC of fruit/animals and add to it as topic develops ... Collect food labels. Taste fruit ... observe. Make a fruit salad? Which fruits have come from Africa?	Basket of fruit. Toys (zoo) animals, puppets African Animals ABC (Browne 1994)	Do they show some awareness of the world beyond and other cultures? What do individual children contribute to discussions? Personal responses from the children. Do children ask questions to gain or extend knowledge? Can
3 Elephants – through a focus on the story of The Hunter (Geraghty 1999)	Caring for wild animals (danger of extinction/ danger of poachers ... survival. Lions ... African/Indian elephants.	Read The Hunter. Share and discuss the main focus story. Paint a picture of the story.	Big Book – fiction and non-fiction The Hunter (Geraghty 1999) Bashi, Elephant Baby (Radcliffe 1984)	children select appropriate colours and materials to make a chosen animal or mask?
4 Elmer stories (McKee 1998)	Variety of life – different animals. Links with the literacy hour	Links with the Literacy Hour – fact and fiction. Activities to explore shape, pattern and colour	Selection of Elmer stories (McKee 1998) soft Elmer toy. Collage materials. Story of The Greedy Zebra (Hadithi 1984)	Do they recognize similarities and differences between a variety of animals. Can they differentiate?
5 Other African animals – through 'Rumble in the Jungle' (Andreae 1996) 6 Walking through the Jungle (Lacombe 1993)		Links with the Literacy Hour ... 'Animal Safari' role play ... Make animal masks. Independent writing on animal shapes. Sort farm and wild animals	Zoo and farm. Small world play. Large wild animals	Children recognize features of living things ... look closely at similarities, differences, patterns

Table 2.4 Reception class teachers' medium-term plans linked to areas of learning (DFEE/QCA 2000a)

	Summer term Topic: Africa		
Personal and Social	**Creative**	**Physical**
Respect for cultures and beliefs of others	*Explore colour, texture, shape, form and space in 2D and 3D*	*Movement*
• Sharing stories • Visitors	• Hot colours • Pattern/colour in the environment/in materials • Animal masks • Weaving to make a basket	• Positional words – Walking in the Jungle • Like an animal • Dance
Feelings	*Music*	*Keeping healthy*
• Story *The Hunter* – share and talk about feelings	• Related songs and rhymes • Using instrument to tell Handas surprise • Rhythm work • Listening to African drummer – make a simple drum • Carnival of animals	• How to keep safe in the sun
Caring for living things	*Movement*	*Large apparatus*
	• Move to drums – respond to • Like the animals	• Explore movement – positional words
	Small world play	*Small apparatus*
	• Zoo/farm animals	• Handa balanced the basket on her head. Balance work using beanbags
	Role-play area	*Malleable materials*
	• Safaris bus Garden centre • Suitable tools in area	• Make an elephant/animal in playdough • Rolling to make a long snake
	Design and making	
	• Make a drum	

Table 2.4 (continued)

Summer term Topic: Africa

Language and Literacy	Mathematics	Knowledge and Understanding
Speaking/listening	*Measures*	*Look closely at . . . Pattern/similarities and differences*
• Discussion about the continent, shape, size	• Comparative language big/small, tall/short, heavy/light, fast/slow	• Animals/camouflage
• Extend vocabulary		• Home and Africa
• Related poems and rhymes	*Shape and space*	*Features of living things*
Reading	• Patterns in the environment/animals/ culture	• African animals
• Information books	• Shapes	• Fruit
• Labels/posters	• Tessellation/pattern of Elmer	*Investigate using senses*
• African alphabet	• Positional words – small world play	• Fruit food from Africa
Writing	*Tallying*	• Listening to African drummer
• For paintings	• Graph of favourite animal	• Looking at pattern
• Animal descriptions	*Numbers*	*Culture and beliefs of others*
• Descriptive on animal shapes	• Dot to dot to 20	• African stories
• Phonic work	• Count in 2's	• Drama work
Role play	*Adding and subtracting*	*Tools and techniques*
• Area to be set up as Garden centre/safari bus	• Related to *Handa's Surprise*	• Make a drum following visitor
• Writing postcards	Related number rhymes/songs/stories	• Junk models of animals
• Passports		• Making masks

Table 2.5 Medium-term plans: Ghana, Years 1/2

	Learning objectives	Activities	Outcomes	Cross-curricular links
1	• To describe perceptions of life in a village in Ghana (Chereponi) • To develop questions about a distant locality	Parcel of Ghanaian and UK artefacts (e.g. cocoa beans, fabric, drums with Africa print pattern, home made money box, oil lamps). What does this tell you about the place it comes from?	Children • Can sort artefacts into categories: Ghana/UK • Can explain what they think each object tells them about the place it comes from • Identify similarities and differences	Music Introduction to African drumming
2	• To draw what it may be like to live in this place, based on information in pictures • To consider how it is different from our town	In pairs children look at pictures of an aspect of life in Ghanaian village, (Chereponi) and similar picture of local area. Part of each picture covered Describe what you can see; draw what is covered; compare	Children • Express and test their perceptions of life in Ghana village • Describe similarities and differences between this and their experiences	Music Introduction to African drumming
3	• To find Africa on a globe • To find Ghana on a map • To find Chereponi on large scale map • To make observations about where things are located in the village • Demonstrate ability to use a key	• Lay out photographs on floor; link with string to local map. • Use bricks representing buildings/features on map	Children • Have enhanced understanding of use of globes and maps of different scales • Can make model of village • Can describe locations of features in and around village	Making 'African' colours
4	• To ask questions about life in Ghanaian village and communicate findings in different ways	• Listen to story of life in a family in the village (Action Aid resources) • Make up own stories about life in the village	Children Ask about and answer questions about life in a Ghanaian village and communicate in role play, pictures or writing	Story writing
5	• To begin to develop a sense of place	In pairs look at photograph of an aspect of life in a Ghanaian village. (Chereponi) Compare with a similar activity in UK (e.g. children's games, preparing food, growing food, fuel, building materials	Whole class can create composite descriptions and comparisons	Making African prints

Resources:
Rural Development Education, Development Education Centre, Birmingham. AKLOWA, Takely House, Brewers End Takely Bishop Stortford, Herts CM22 6QJ; Action Aid, Ghana, Chataway House, Leach Road, Chard, Somerset, TH20 1FA. Teacher's Resource Packs, Africa, Drums. African masks, The Adinkra cloth of Ghana

Table 2.6 Analysis of the ways in which work in each area of learning at the Foundation Stage is developed through work in each subject at Key Stage 1 of the National Curriculum

Subject	Foundation Stage	Key Stage 1
Music	• Recognize and explore how sounds can be changed; sing simple songs from memory, recognize repeated sounds and sound patterns and match movements to music • Use imagination in music, dance	• Use voices – sing songs, chants • Play tuned and untuned instruments • Release and perform with others • Create musical patterns • Explore, choose and organise sounds and musical ideas
Geography	• Have a developing respect for their own cultures and beliefs and for those of others • Look closely at similarities and differences	• Ask geographical questions e.g. what is it like to live in this place? • Use globes, maps and secondary sources of information • Identify and describe what places are like • Recognise how places compare with other places; how places are linked to other places e.g. food from other countries • Study a contrasting locality outside the UK
PSE	• Understand that people have different views, cultures and beliefs • Understand what is right, what is wrong and why; consider consequences of words and actions • Work as part of a group	• Recognise what is fair and unfair • Share opinions and exchange views • Take part in discussions • Recognise how their behaviour affects others • Consider social and moral dilemmas

Table 2.6 (continued)

Subject	Foundation Stage	Key Stage 1
Communication, language and literacy	• Interact with others, negotiating plans and activities, taking turns in conversation • Extend vocabulary	• Speak clearly, fluently, confidently, with appropriate intonation, organize what they say, focus on main points, include relevant detail, take into account needs of listeners
Speaking and listening	• Speak clearly and audibly with confidence and control	• Listen, understand, remember specific points, listen to others reactions, take different views into account, extend ideas, give reasoning for opinions
Drama	• Tell narratives in correct sequence • Enjoy spoken language and reading turn to it in play and listening	• Tell stories • Listen to adults
Drama	• Use language to imagine and recreate roles and experiences • Use talk to organize, sequence and clarify thinking, ideas, feelings, events • Use imagination in imaginative role play and stories	• Use language and actions to explore situations, characters, emotions • Create and sustain roles individually and when working with others • Comment continually on drama they have taken part in • Work in role • Present drama and stories to others • Respond to performance
Reading	• Show understanding of elements of stories: main characters, sequence of events	• Develop understanding of fiction and drama from a range of cultures – identify and describe characters, events, settings • Express preferences, give reasons • Act out stories • Respond imaginatively in different ways

Table 2.6 (continued)

Subject	Foundation Stage	Key Stage I
Information and communication technology	• Use information and communication technology to support learning	• Share ideas by presenting information in a variety of ways • Present completed work effectively • Review what they have done to help them develop their ideas • Talk about what they might change in future work
Art and design	• Explore colour, texture, shape • Use imagination in art and design	• Record from imagination and explore ideas • Develop ideas • Investigate possibilities of range of materials and processes • Try out tools and techniques • Represent observations, ideas and feelings • Review what they and others have done and identify what they might change • Learning about colour, pattern, texture • Differences and similarities in work of artists and craft people in different times and cultures • Explore a range of starting points e.g. music, stories • Collaborate with others • Investigate different levels of art, craft, design

Introduction:
an empty canvas

THE SCHOOLS

Brantwood Nursery School and Clappersgate Primary School are in the centre of a large market town near the river, close to the large parish church built on profits from the medieval wool trade and the busy, mainly eighteenth-century, main shopping street. You can look out across large estates of both privately owned and council houses, where most of the Brantwood and Clappersgate families live, to the fells beyond.

Clappersgate is a two-storey school solidly built in 1698 in local limestone. It has been much added to over the years, most recently with classrooms for reception and Key Stage 1. The head teacher, Peter Soames, had joined the school two years earlier. Previously he had been head of a large inner city primary school in the north of England, and he brought with him a commitment to offering children an added dimension to their education through a range of opportunities. These included a wide range of extra-curricular activities and a variety of partnerships, which provided learning opportunities for children and developed school–community links. Partners ranged from a group of European schools, local businesses, an after school care club, other local schools, voluntary organizations and a teacher training college. These partnerships, in addition to providing a range of learning opportunities and developing community links, did a great deal for the development and celebration of the school ethos and identity. After ten years at his previous school Peter moved to Clappersgate seeking a new challenge in a different environment.

There are fourteen classes at Clappersgate and seventeen teachers. Sue Curran and Sue Hodgson teach the reception classes; Lydia Bradley and Linda Melrose teach the Year 1 classes and Fran Bailey and Pat Spencer teach Year 2. Kirsty Klijn, who coordinated the project, teaches Year 3. Most of the staff have lived in the area for many years and are experienced in teaching Key Stage 1.

Brantwood is a local authority nursery school with three classes of twenty-five four-year-olds. The head teacher is Sue Markham. The teacher who coordinated the project in the Nursery School was Veronica Boles, working with the nursery nurse Jane Lambert. Toddlers' groups are held for an hour each afternoon for about twelve two-year-olds with their parents, in preparation for joining the nursery. The school is situated in a spacious three-storey Victorian house and has a homely feel. In the large garden children can set off on 'sea adventures' in an old upturned boat, defend the fort which is reached by a 'perilous' rope bridge, help tend the garden, and play in the sand hut.

The teachers particularly wanted to work with us during the summer term because that is when the nursery school children are prepared for their move to Clappersgate, 'real school'. The reception teachers, Sue Curran and Sue Hodgson, would be making visits to talk to the Brantwood staff, to meet the children who would be moving on to the reception class and to plan the visits the children and their parents would be making to Clappersgate. This would provide a sound basis for the project; it could create a purposeful context for the nursery children and their parents to visit Clappersgate. The college had worked in partnership with both Brantwood and Clappersgate for many years, supporting the school-based work of student teachers, and, extending this connection, we had worked together on other literacy, history, mathematics and drama projects (Cooper 1999; Cooper and Etches 1996; Foster 2000; Toye 2000). 'It's so good for the children', one of the teachers said. 'They couldn't believe that it was them on the cover – in colour!' So, on a sunny early spring afternoon at the end of March five tutors – Nigel Toye (drama), Liz Elliott and Pete Saunders (both information and communication technology), Andrea Brook (art), Kath Langley-Hamel (English), and Hilary Cooper, who was coordinating the project, had a first meeting with the Brantwood and Clappersgate teachers.

THE ARTS

The focus originally planned for the second part of our project was 'the arts': drama, music, painting and printing. Nigel Toye had been working with the head teacher, Sue Markham, and Veronica Boles at Brantwood Nursery School during the previous term, exploring the development of communication and social skills in very young children, through drama with the teacher in role. Sue and Veronica were keen to build on this and to extend it across reception and Key Stage 1. The music strand was led by Kirsty Klijn, a Year 3 teacher at Clappersgate who had been a specialist music student at college several years previously. Kirsty is also seconded to work with tutors in college one morning a week on Year 3 of the Education Studies BA/QTS course. Being a teacher at Clappersgate, she undertook a large share of the project management. The research project budget provided funding for supply cover so that she could work in Brantwood Nursery School before the formal beginning of the project and become familiar with the school and the children. Andrea Brook had previously been art coordinator in a large international school and welcomed the chance to work again with a teachers in schools.

PLANNING THE PROJECT

We met in Pat Spencer's room, always an inspirational place. When I am there it reminds me of why I had first wanted to work with young children. In one corner was a 'rock cave', overhung with branches of leaves suspended from a net – a calm, quiet place where children could lose themselves in the magic of stories about islands. The imaginary island of *Miranda the Castaway* (Mayhew 1997) blends with the real island of Struig, the setting for the Katie Morag stories (Hedderwick 1984). The rest of the room interweaves fantasy and reality: make-believe treasure maps and real routes based on maps of Struig; letters in bottles sent from their own island cave, and stories inspired by both Katie Morag and Miranda. 'The cave is on the island of Barra', Pat explained. 'We're finding out about Barra as a contrasting locality in the British Isles. In Year 1 they found out about our locality and now we're comparing life in our town with life on a Hebridean island. The Katie Morag books are a good way in because the illustrations are geographically accurate.'

The teachers wanted to use the project to do things: to make the children's leap from nursery to 'real school' successful and to work on a theme which would take them beyond Europe. In the previous week, after a college lecture on the subject of cultural diversity, Kirsty had led a seminar in which student teachers considered ways in which children in monocultural schools can, in spite of their own (and perhaps the teachers') limited direct experience, enjoy and benefit from a culturally diverse curriculum. She had continued this conversation with her colleagues back in school.

Clappersgate teachers talked about how they had previously worked very successfully with a black African musician from Soweto, Raymond Takalani Otto, and his possible willingness to participate. Raymond runs the Takalani Dance Theatre, which offers a wide range of workshops not only within schools and colleges but also within community and theatre venues. Kirsty showed us his leaflet:

> South Africa is home to a vibrant, diverse culture where the air is alive with a variety of music styles, rhythms, dance and colour. If I can contribute to building multicultural awareness and touch the lives of others through my work then I will be happy that I have achieved something.

'Africa' caught everyone's imagination. Raymond Otto was considered ideal to work with nursery and Key Stage 1 on rhythm and dance. The nursery teachers decided this was a good idea and that it could easily be adopted throughout the school for the first four weeks of the summer term. Although Clappersgate staff had already agreed their medium-term plans, the teachers began to suggest ways in which these could be modified to incorporate an African theme.

SATS (Standard Assessment Tasks) in mathematics and English for Year 2 children take place towards the end of June, and every morning is scheduled for work on these two subjects. Pat Spencer can always be relied on for an upbeat response. 'How marvellous!' she exclaimed. 'What rich afternoons we shall have! African art and drama and songs and dance and stories. Wonderful!' The college tutors ideas started to fizz, too. 'Africa with three-year-olds – hot colours – that's the first thing I think of', said Andrea. 'Lots of African stories', said Kath. Nigel was initially disappointed that the drama he had hoped to do based on Little Bo-Peep would not fit into the African theme, but then someone pointed out that this was a timely change of plan: the appalling outbreak of foot-and-mouth disease in Cumbria had devastated some local families, and a tale of losing a sheep was a story suddenly too close to home for the three-year-olds.

SOME CONCERNS

Then individuals began to voice concerns:

> What do we mean by 'Africa?' Africa is a vast continent with many diverse cultures and climates and landscapes . . .

> Are we talking about modern cities or traditional villages? Which villages?

> Do we mean exotic images of Africa, or do we mean poverty, wars, sickness?

> Why should nursery children – or even six-year-olds – learn about Africa when they don't know much about their own street?

These questions made us think more carefully about 'Africa' and the connotations of our project.

RESOLUTIONS

Gradually we teased out that what we especially wanted to introduce the children to was traditional African stories, art and music. These things are universal, with roots both in Africa and the children's immediate experience. Storytelling is an integral part of the African and the oral tradition. Anthony Enahoro, son of a schoolmaster in West Africa, has described his own experience:

> Those young children of a very large family, who were not already asleep, lay on mats listening to stories told by the women of the household. Such stories might be folklore, myth or history, and such themes had been enacted thousands of times in every family of the Ishan tribe from time immemorial.
>
> (Hulton 1998: 83)

Many traditional tales are shared across cultures. They may be told in different cultural contexts and so illustrated by different images, which extend the imagination and both enrich and challenge children's own limited experience of life, but children also understand and respond to them because they are about our common human and moral predicaments, and we can recognize them. 'For example, in *Handa's Surprise*,' Veronica said, 'Handa, a little African girl, puts seven fruits in her basket to take as a gift to her friend Akeyo. They are fruits English children recognize: a banana a pineapple, an orange. . . . As she walks to the next village each fruit is stolen by an animal, also recognized by the children from pictures or the zoo: a monkey, a zebra, an elephant, a giraffe . . . lots of rich colours and brush strokes that zap each scene into life. Children enjoy the jokes, the repetition, the sequence of the story. Everything seems to be going wrong as the basket empties, and there is no fruit for Akeyo – *then* – a goat knocks all the tangerines off a tree and into the basket, which is full again!'

Kirsty pointed out that many children find it easy to relate to and enjoy African song and rhythm through their own musical experiences: from the early days of singing and clapping, tapping toys, tubs and pans, and taking pleasure in the sounds produced. Children also naturally link movement with music from playground clapping/singing games to a natural instinct to move to music, particularly rhythmic and upbeat music. And decorative textiles, Andrea explained, have been at the heart of all societies at all times in the form of clothes, furnishings and art – with Africa providing some outstanding examples of textile design, the printed Adinka cloth of Ghana for example.

We were reassured. After all, as someone remembered reading in *The Times Educational Supplement*, the Horniman Museum in south London had planned an ambitious educational project for younger children involving art,

ICT, literacy and citizenship inspired by the African World exhibition. Children were going to work with museum staff, storytellers, poets and textile artists to explore African artefacts on display. 'We'll see what we can do up north', we declared. By 5.30 the teachers had agreed to include 'Africa' in their medium-term plans for the first four weeks of the summer term. Each would make detailed arrangements with a college tutor as to how the work would be taken forward.

MEDIUM-TERM PLANS

The nursery teachers incorporated Africa within their intended topic on food. Table 2.1 shows how the focus moved from familiar food at home, in week 1, to eating in other places (with a McDonald's role-play area) in week 2. In week 3 food in an African context would be introduced through story and role play, leading into African art, in the fourth week.

Table 2.2 shows how the weekly focuses in the nursery were linked to areas of learning (QCA/DFEE 2000). This draft was developed into detailed plans for each area of learning,

Table 2.3 shows the reception class teachers' plan for the Africa theme and Table 2.4 how this was linked to areas of learning. In Years 1 and 2, work was planned for each subject separately. Table 2.5 shows a medium-term plan for a geography topic on Ghana based on the format of the QCA schemes of work. Table 2.6 analyses the way in which work in each area at the Foundation Stage is developed through work in each subject at Key Stage 1, based on the guidance for the Foundation Stage (QCA/DFEE 2000) and in the National Curriculum.

BIBLIOGRAPHY

Browne, E. (1997) *Handa's Surprise*, London: Walker Books.
Hedderwick, M. (1984) *Katie Morag Delivers the Mail*, London: Bodley Head.
Hulton, M. (1998) 'African Traditional Stories in the Classroom'. in D. Atkinson (ed) *The Children's Bookroom: Reading and the use of Books*. Stoke on Trent: Trentham.
Mayhew, J. (1997) *Miranda the Castaway*, London: Dolphin.
McKee, D. (1998) *Elmer*, London: Redfox

Chapter 6

Music: feel the beat

Kirsty Klijn

CONTEXT

The music element of this study aimed to explore ways in which the subject could be taught from nursery through reception and Years 1 and 2. As a teacher at Clappersgate Primary School I was able to further links with Brantwood Nursery School and explore areas connected with existing medium-term plans for each year group. I began the project by spending time in Brantwood to enable me to get to know the pupils and staff better. This allowed the children to be more relaxed when they worked with me. Time spent in discussion with Sue Markham and the other teachers from the nursery, and with Sue Curran and Sue Hodgson, the reception teachers, provided opportunities for sharing ideas and focused our thoughts on ways to provide a smooth transition across the crucial Foundation Stage.

The chosen topic – Africa – offered a great deal of scope for introducing children to African music and developing their rhythmic skills. I was keen to ensure that the planned lessons were firmly rooted in the music curriculum, with these aims being explored through the topic work. There is a danger when undertaking a topic-based approach that the topic can become dominant rather than merely the vehicle through which the objectives can be explored.

Another element of the project was to involve visitors and the wider community. The Takalini Dance Theatre, run by Raymond Otto, was invited to conduct workshops with the children from nursery to Year 2. Raymond visits schools to run a wide range of workshops based on South African culture. On this occasion the focus was drumming/rhythm work and dance. The day culminated in a whole-school performance to which the nursery children's parents were invited.

THE PLANNING STAGE

The planning stage began with discussions between the teachers from Brantwood Nursery, the reception teachers and myself. Medium-term plans were shared and initial ideas for the music element discussed. It was important to make the links with the children's experiences explicit rather than merely 'do' abstract activities. A way of achieving this was through using a book that was familiar to the children as a focus to give structure to the musical activities.

Due to the younger age and shorter attention span of the nursery children, it was agreed that the sessions would involve small groups of around ten and last for only ten minutes. This would enable the children to get the most out of the sessions. Each group would then have a follow-up session a week after Raymond Otto's visit, to reinforce and extend the activities. In the reception classes, the session would be for longer and involve the whole class, as it would for the other sessions in Year 1 and Year 2. As the school has a two-form entry it was decided that each class would be involved in a single session so that every class would have some input.

The next stage in the planning process involved matching the initial ideas and medium-term plans provided by the teachers, together with the *National Curriculum* (DFEE 1999), *QCA Schemes of Work for Music* (QCA 2000a) and *Curriculum Guidance for the Foundation Stage* (QCA 2000b). The 'stepping stones' in the *Curriculum Guidance for the Foundation Stage* provided an important link in terms of progression of skills between nursery and reception. For Years 1 to 6 the school had an overall framework identifying the aspects of music studied each term, drawing from the QCA music schemes as guidance.

TRACKING THROUGH THE PROGRESSION

There were three strands running through the objectives set for each of the year groups. These strands are examined in turn to illustrate how they progressed from nursery to Year 3. The first strand was to listen and respond to music from the African culture. In terms of QCA this would be an example of an 'ongoing skill,' and one that is a vital element to the musical experiences of young children.

> The younger the child, the more open he or she is to unfamiliar music. So KS 1 and the early part of KS 2 should use as wide a range of different kinds of music as possible.
>
> (QCA 2000b)

In terms of the stepping stones for the Foundation Stage, this strand enables children to 'respond to sound with body movement' (yellow), 'imitate and create movement in response to music' (blue), 'begin to move rhythmically' (green), leading to the early learning goal 'match movements to music'.

In the lessons themselves, this strand took the form of the children listening to short extracts of African music and responding in some way. The younger ones were encouraged to respond through tapping and simple body percussion to the beat. The older children were encouraged to listen more carefully to features such as who was singing, whether it was accompanied and whether they could identify any repeating patterns. There is a lot of scope for this type of short listening activity to be incorporated into the school day; it can be used instead of story or as part of a movement lesson, not just in a 'music lesson'.

The second strand involved listening to and copying musical patterns. Starting with a basic level of tapping back a simple rhythm, this aspect is identified through the blue stepping stone: 'tap out simple repeated rhythms and make some up'. This was developed with the older children to give them an opportunity to lead the activity: improvising their own patterns for others to copy, an example of a 'disciplined skill'. This skill was developed through a game where the children were challenged to follow and join in repeated rhythmic patterns, then to repeat back simple rhythms, progressing to more complex rhythms involving rests, patterns linking pitch and rhythms, and finally a memory game where rhythmic patterns had to be memorized and then repeated back after an interval.

This type of activity needs to be used for short bursts, regularly, to build up the children's skills. I have used it successfully as a warm-up activity to begin the music lesson and at the end of lesson as a whole-class activity. It can also work well as a 'fill-in', such as in the five minutes before a break time, waiting for the last few children to get changed for PE, at the end or start of the day.

The final strand was to structure sounds, which included working with sounds within a structure. With the younger children, a book formed the basis for this work. Books for younger children usually have a clear structure, often with some repetition of ideas and language. The children were introduced to the book on an earlier occasion so that they were familiar with the story. This allowed the musical aspects to be a major focus.

These three strands were used for the purpose of this study to illustrate the ways in which progression of skills is possible in music from nursery to Year 3. It is suggested, however, that the practitioner focuses on only one or two areas for each of their music lessons.

PROVIDING A STRUCTURE

Each session was based on either a book or a song to provide a focus and structure. The big book *Walking Through the Jungle* (Lacombe 1993) was decided on after discussion with the nursery and reception teachers as it employed a simple language structure involving a lot of repetition and gave scope for building a sequence of sounds to represent different animals. Aspects of the stepping stones related to this are: 'show an interest in the way musical instruments sound' (yellow) and 'explore the sounds of different instruments' (green). Although the initial work involved structuring the sounds using the book, later work could involve children using the sounds to compose their own sequences. One way of managing this is to provide the sound makers and sound cue cards in an area of the classroom to be used by groups and individuals at a time other than the set music lesson. This allows children to reflect on and explore the sequencing work started in the lesson and can encourage more timid children to have a go.

A similarly structured book, which Veronica had talked about at our initial meeting, *Handa's Surprise* (Browne 1994), was used with the reception classes. This contained language that was slightly more advanced language but still involved repetition, since the story involved a young African girl called Handa who decided to take a basket of fruit to her friend and various animals steal the items of fruit along the way. The story gave scope for sequencing sounds for each piece of fruit being stolen. It also offered the opportunity to include a pulse for the steady walking of Handa along her journey. An element of surprise was also incorporated when a goat knocks a tree, causing the empty basket to fill with tangerines.

In Year 1, a simple song with repeated lines provided the structure and enabled the children to join in the end of each line in a simple question-and-answer type activity. A rhythmic section was then interspersed into the melody. The rhythm was based on the words of the song, and as the song built up, untuned percussion instruments were introduced in sequence. There was scope in follow-up sessions for the children to build their own sequences, composing additional lines to be used in the song.

A song was also used in Year 2 to provide a structure. This time the pupils used the song to explore a tune repeated at different pitches: first low, then middle, then high and finally returning to low. The rhythm of the song followed the African words and was more complex than that used with Year 1. Body percussion was used to accompany the rhythm. Follow-up work using tuned percussion would give the children an opportunity to explore this further.

The planned lessons in Years 1 and 2 show how links between aspects of music can be exploited. The rhythmic focus of the Year 1 work related to work on pulse and rhythm. The work on pitch with the Year 2 pupils linked to previous work on pitch and the reinforcement of ostinati. Visual cues can be used to support the children's concept of structures. These visual cues could be a book, such as those used with the nursery and reception classes. Alternatively, they may take the form of flashcards bearing words, pictures, drawings of instruments or even simple musical notation: for example, a picture cue with the speech ostinato and notation written underneath. Teacher and pupil can use these to change existing sequences or compose new musical sequences. The following sections outline the observations made from the sessions themselves.

The nursery

The work undertaken in the nursery school followed several previous visits to meet with the pupils and staff and get a feel for the type of learning environment the children were used to. Brantwood Nursery School provided a wide range of creative topic-related activities for the children to engage in; for example, tasting a variety of dishes from different countries as a way of leading into thinking how people from other countries might live.

The music sessions took place in a 'family room' and provided a quiet, calm environment allowing the children to focus on the musical activities. There was ample space to seat them all and lay out a variety of instruments, cue flashcards and a big book on a stand. Either the class teacher or a classroom assistant accompanied each group and helped by making a video record of the sessions. The analysis that follows is based on field notes and the video record.

The first sessions were with two groups of ten who attended the nursery in the afternoons. In the second set of sessions, the children were more familiar with the activities and with me, and therefore more responsive. Those who had been present at both sessions were clearly more confident and willing to suggest ideas than others who had only attended one. This emphasizes the importance of regular musical activity with young children.

Listening to the African music, all the children demonstrated an awareness and enjoyment of moving to it, with some of them able to tap along to the beat for short periods of time. If continued as a short-burst activity over time, this skill would develop further. Follow-up to this activity would be to use a larger space to further explore moving to a beat. It is through this moving to and 'feeling' the beat that children develop their sense of rhythm and pulse.

The aim of the work based on *Walking Through the Jungle* by Julie Lacombe was not to produce sound effects for each animal but to focus the children's listening and thoughts on how different instruments produced different sorts of sounds: some loud, some soft, just as the animals made different sounds, some loud and some soft. These sounds could then be used for the sequencing activity.

The children were clear that the lion would make a loud sound. Jenny, who had some castanets, said, 'These make a loud sound and so these might make a lion sound.' She proceeded to shake them so the others could hear the sound. At this age, children often use practical demonstration to explain their ideas. When we discussed which sound to have for the snake, Danny knew the maracas would make a soft sound like the hissing of a snake and pointed to them, saying excitedly, 'I . . . I . . . watch', and played them to illustrate his idea.

In addition to thinking about loud and soft, some instruments allowed the children to also consider the duration of the sound it made. When I played the large cymbal, they listened intently to the length of sound it produced, showing real amazement when it finally stopped ringing. Although this was unplanned, I wanted to pick up on this response and encouraged them to listen again whilst wiggling their fingers until they could no longer hear the cymbal. This was to reinforce their listening and highlight the length of time the sound could be heard. This type of short focused activity can be found in *Gently Into Music* (York 1984).

During the second session, the activities were revisited and extended. This repetition enabled some of the quieter children to make suggestions about the sounds the instruments made. They were also able to listen to other people's ideas and agree or disagree. When asked about an instrument to suggest a 'Grrrr', James suggested the cymbal, which was then played to the group. As soon as they heard the sudden loud crash of the cymbal and long ringing that followed, most of the group, including James himself, shook their heads, saying 'No'. Finally the guiro was scraped slowly and the children agreed that it matched the 'Grrrr' more closely. It is in this type of informal exploration of instruments that the concepts of musical elements, timbre, volume and duration can start to be developed.

Picture cue cards of the animals were used to help the group sequence the sounds with the story. These were also used as a means of introducing the children to the idea of building their own sequence. A volunteer was chosen and asked to sequence three cards. The children who played the instruments which represented those sounds then played when their card was pointed to. This is the very beginning of composing.

Summary

- Exploit the movement and music links to develop a sense of pulse and rhythm.
- Maintain pace and variety of activities in sessions, revisit and build on over a series of weeks, keeping each session short.
- Explore the children's responses where relevant, even if these are unexpected and not in the plan.

Reception

During the warm-up game all the children were able to copy a repeating pattern and the majority able to clap back simple rhythms. This showed a development from the nursery children, of whom only a few in each group were secure in repeating a rhythm or repeating pattern. During the listening element whole-body movement was even more in evidence, with children nodding heads and swaying as well as tapping in time with the beat. Again, picture cue cards were used to help the children structure the sounds with the book. The children were more independent in following these with the book and did not require prompts from the teacher pointing at the cards for them to play their part.

This activity could be followed up and developed further by getting the children to work individually or in pairs to make their own music for each cue card. For example, a short tune or rhythm could be used for when the pineapple is stolen, perhaps even using the word 'pineapple' to give the rhythm.

Children were more confident in their handling of instruments: finding techniques to make the best sounds for each, such as ensuring the cymbal dangled freely so that the sound was not dampened. This suggested that when children are given opportunities to explore playing instruments in the Foundation Stage they quickly become confident in knowing how to get the most pleasing sounds from them.

When I introduced the repeating rhythm of Handa, I allowed the children time just to listen and then join in when they had 'caught' the beat. It is important for children to be given this time to absorb the beat and to join in only once they feel ready to, otherwise they end up playing catch-up or lose the beat very quickly.

It was clear that the children had a clear grasp of how the musical ideas connected with the story. When questioned, they suggested the walking idea should carry on throughout the story. Upon further questioning as to why it should do so, Katie said, 'Because her friend's house is a long way away.'

Summary

- Give children time to 'catch' the beat.
- Encourage children to follow cue cards independently to help sequence and structure their music.
- Continue to develop children's rhythmic skills through short copying activities, little and often.

Year 1

During the 'copycats' games in the warm-up the rhythms were extended to include more complex ones which made them longer and included some rests. Individual children were then asked to volunteer to 'be the leader' by tapping out their own improvised rhythm on the drum for the rest of the class to copy. Initially unsure, the children soon gained confidence and the class teacher continued this activity later. This allowed the children to rapidly become secure at improvising rhythms over a short period of time.

Then the children were introduced to the song and taught an ending to each line. This was repeated three times in a 'question and answer' style before the final line that had a slightly different 'question' melody. Despite the difference in the final line being so subtle, some children were able to identify the change and said, 'It was different.'

Musical skills develop at different rates in different children, and this often provides an opportunity for those who may not excel in other areas to really shine. One example of this was a child with learning and behavioural difficulties who was very soon able to maintain a complex syncopated rhythm securely, well before many of the others had picked it up. Without regular opportunities for creative activities such as music, children are not given the full opportunity to explore and celebrate their potential.

A rhythmic interlude between repeats was introduced through the words of the song. This rhythm was developed from the speech to body percussion to untuned percussion – a useful process in developing children's rhythmic skills.

Summary

- Once children are secure with copying simple rhythms extend the activity; e.g. use more complex rhythms, encourage children to improvise their own rhythms.
- Words can be used to provide a scaffold for rhythms; use the words of a song to support the playing of a rhythm as an accompaniment.
- Ensure high pupil involvement to maximize the children's opportunity to *make* music. Use body percussion if too many instruments are likely to spoil the effect or if resources are not available.

Year 2

The warm up game was further extended and adapted with the Year 2 classes by singing the rhythms to high and low pitches. This reinforced the previous term's focus on pitch. Hand signals were used to give a visual cue to the pitch, and these were quickly picked up by the children, many of whom used them in their responses.

The class were introduced to the song which involved one line of melody being repeated at different pitches before returning to the original. They were quick to identify the structure. 'It keeps going around', Nadim commented. This indicated a good grasp of pitch and structure with the tune returning to its 'home' note each time. There are close links between music and movement. The exploitation of these links impact on children's musical and movement development:

- Music and movement can reflect and reinforce one another.
- Movement has the great advantage of involving the whole body, and so the whole being, of the child. (Flash 1993: 87).

A simple sequence of movement was introduced to highlight the strong beats and rests in the African song used with Year 2. This involved the children in whole-body movement that could accompany and reinforce the rhythm of the song. A word of caution: care needs to be taken when planning movement within a music lesson to ensure the movement enhances the music rather than detracts from it.

The class teachers used a video of a performance from the Gambia as a follow-up. This demonstrated how a group of musicians in Africa used movement to emphasize the rhythmic nature of their song. A more advanced level of listening was evident with these older children, with many of them identifying features of the music – for example, whether it was accompanied – and starting to copy the clicking rhythm featured in the extract.

Summary

- A complexity of rhythms and the use of pitch can be used to extend copying-type activities.
- Exploit opportunities to link movement and music so as to enhance the children's grasp of musical elements and their range of response.
- The same extract of music can be used throughout the Foundation Stage and Key Stage 1, with children responding at their own level.
- The rhythm game can be further adapted in Key Stage 2 by incorporating a higher degree of musical memory in the game 'Switch'.
- Develop the sequencing work by combining rhythms/melodies played by groups instead of having one follow the other in turn.
- Extend the complexity of the parts by transferring musical ideas to body percussion, untuned percussion and tuned percussion.

THE RAYMOND OTTO EXPERIENCE

An important element of the project was the aim of involving the wider community and visitors in the creative arts. The workshop brought together elements covered in the music sessions. It provided the children with an opportunity to play 'real' African drums to develop their sense of rhythm and to learn dance sequences in preparation for a whole-school performance at the end of the day. A day such as this has many highlights, many instances where individuals can excel. One particular example was that of a child with behavioural difficulties who led the dance in front of the whole school. He seemed almost completely unaware of the audience as he was so totally absorbed in his movement to the music.

The final performance also allowed the rest of the school to share in a musical experience with the nursery, reception and Year 1 and 2 children, together with the parents of nursery children. At one point every person in the hall, nearly five hundred people, was enjoying and sharing in moving to music.

CONCLUSION

The project has demonstrated a wide variety of ways in which music through a topic can be used to develop skills in nursery age children through to Year 2. Some aspects, such as listening to extracts, transfer directly across age groups, with children accessing them at their own level. Other aspects, such as the listening to and copying of patterns, needed some adjustment depending on the age and experiences of the children.

It was clear from completing the project that the topic-based concept allowed links to be made across the age range and musical experiences to be shared and celebrated, whilst developing specific musical skills at each age.

There are numerous ways in which the musical activities described could be used with different groups of children and related to different topics. They offer starting points to be explored and developed within the changing context of the classroom.

Finally, a key message from the project was how the process of observation should never be underestimated by all those involved in teaching, in particular, the observation of a specialist working in any field, regardless of the stage of their career. While this chapter has provided one example within a particular context, it is no substitute for simply watching teachers teach.

FOLLOW-UP IDEAS

- Rehearse and polish before performing for others.
- Try letting different children play the drum and/or percussion.
- Divide the children into groups, e.g. the band who play instruments, the singers and dancers or 'movers'.
- Leave a xylophone or glockenspiel in the classroom for the children to try picking out the song or accompaniment.
- Set up a listening centre for the children to listen to African music or listen to the tape of the session and then draw or write about it.
- Try out some of the lessons described in the project. The lesson plans are given below.

Brantwood Nursery

This lesson is to be developed over two separate sessions.

Aims

- To be introduced to some African music and respond;
- To copy a rhythmic pattern;
- To create sounds to accompany a story.

Preparation

- Be familiar with the book *Walking Through the Jungle*.

Warm-up

- Sit in a circle. Play 'Follow me' with body percussion. Try to follow the beat and very simple repeating rhythms.
- Listen to some African music with a strong beat and try to join in following the beat by gently tapping different body parts. Stop the music; then play again and see if the children can move to the beat independently.

Main lesson

- Remind children of the book *Walking Through the Jungle*. Ask the children to recall the names of the different animals in the book.
- Ask the children to suggest the sounds made by these animals, saying whether they are loud or quiet.
- Look at the selection of instruments in the centre of the circle. Play each and listen to the sound.
- Ask the children to suggest an instrument for each of the animals. Assign a cue card and instrument to each child, allowing each time to play their instrument for the others to listen to.

Whole class

- Read through the story and encourage the children to play their instrument when the story gets to their animal cue card.

The reception class, Clappersgate Primary School

Aims

- To listen and respond to African music;
- To structure sounds to accompany a story;
- To copy a rhythmic pattern.

Preparation

- Be familiar with the story *Handa's Surprise*.

Warm-up

- Sit in a circle in the classroom.
- Play 'Follow Me' with body percussion. Try to follow simple rhythms and rhythms which involve rests.
- Ask a child to volunteer to be the leader.

Main lesson

- Play some African music with a strong rhythm. The teacher models following the beat on different body parts. Children copy. Then the teacher stops and asks the children to continue on their own.
- Remind the children of the story set in Africa (*Handa's Surprise*), using picture cards of the different animals to build a visual structure of the story (monkey, ostrich, zebra, elephant, giraffe, antelope, parrot, goat).
- Ask a volunteer to walk on the spot as Handa did on her journey to Akeyo. The rest watch and tap along in time. Ask two children to play quietly on a drum to show the walking. Should this be all the time or just once? Remind the children of the story and the fact that Handa walks for most of it. Introduce the walking card (picture of Handa).
- Play each of a selection of untuned percussion instruments. Ask children to select instruments for each of the animals from the variety given and ask them to justify their choice. Discuss whether the animal is big/small, fast/slow and whether the sound should be loud/quiet. Group the children depending on their instruments in a semi-circle arrangement so all can see each other.

Whole class

- Tell the story with the sound accompaniment.

Year 1, Clappersgate Primary School (links to QCA Unit 1 and Unit 4, Pulse and rhythm)

Aims

- To listen to African music and identify features;
- To play a rhythmic pattern to accompany a song;
- To copy and improvise a rhythmic pattern.

Warm-up

- Get the children to sit in a circle in the classroom.
- Play 'Follow me' with body percussion. Try to get them to follow simple rhythms and rhythms which involve rests.
- Ask a child to volunteer to be the leader.

Main lesson

- Introduce an African song. Sing the *phrase*; the children repeat it back. Sing the leader part and phrase; all sing. The children add their part by clapping first and then adding their phrase where the claps went.
- Perform the complete song, practise by using different voices (whisper, loud).
- Teacher introduces reprise and children try to repeat back. Practise, add drums to accompany the reprise. Groups of children play the drums and then pass on that so all have a turn. The rest 'play' on body percussion (knees, tummy, chest).
- Perform with the song in between. Continue by introducing tambourines and xylophone (GAC'C).
- Perform the complete song with a reprise played by groups of children.

Whole class

- Play some African music and ask the children to tap along to the rhythm.

Year 2, Clappersgate Primary School (QCA links to Unit 1, Ongoing skills)

Aims

- To get the children to listen and respond to African music and identify certain features;
- To add a simple *ostinato* accompaniment to an African song;
- To copy melodic and rhythmic patterns.

Warm-up

- Follow the leader (teacher). Listen and watch and then copy *rhythmic* patterns, which include *rests* and *quavers*.
- Play above but using *melodic* patterns involving the *minor third* (doorbell). Use words 'high' and 'low' to help discriminate between the two notes.

Main lesson

- Listen to African music involving singing (Track 9, Ladysmith Black Mambazo, 'Abezizive Ngeke Bayiqede')
- Question the children about the music: Who is singing? One person or several? Men/women/children/mixed? Can you tap along? Tell me anything else you notice. How is it different from the singing they do in assembly?
- Explain that they are going to learn to sing an African song. The words look strange to us; they look like this (show a large version of the words).
- Teach the words by asking children to repeat back, vary by using different voices, e.g. whisper, to ensure clear diction.
- Teach the tune by using your hand to help the children pitch; practise several times. Sing and tap along.
- Sing the song standing and demonstrate the clap, clap, clap, thigh, slap in time to the beat. Ask the children to join in.
- Challenge various children to play the beat on a drum.
- Divide the children into three groups, one for each section of the tune. Assign to each a 'leader' who collects a prepared tuned percussion instrument and plays the two notes (D, E, D, D) (F, G, F, F) (A, B, A, A).
- Combine singing, clapping and the tuned accompaniment.

Whole class

- Show children movement to replace the clapping (step R, step L, step R, jump). Perform as a class.

RESOURCES

Raymond Takalini Otto
Takalini Dance Theatre
P.O. Box 66
Leeds
West Yorkshire
LS8 3XU
www.takalini.co.uk

The Best of Ladysmith Black Mambazo, The Star and the Wiseman, London: Polygram, 1998.

RECOMMENDED READING

York, M. (1984) *Gently Into Music*. London: Longman.
    Full of practical ideas for activities to engage young children in musical activity.
Cain, T. and Palmer, J. *Music in the Curriculum* CIHE, Southampton.
    A magazine featuring articles which share varied and practical ideas for music making with children.

BIBLIOGRAPHY

Browne, E. (1994) *Handa's Surprise*, London: Walker Books.
Browne, P.-A. (1995) *African Animals ABC*, Bristol: Barefoot.
Glover, G. and Ward, S. (1993) *Teaching Music in the Primary School*, London: Cassell.
Lacombe, J. (1993) *Walking Through the Jungle*, London: Walker Books.
York, M. (1984) *Gently Into Music*, London: Longman.

Reference was also made to the following DFEE/QCA documents:
(1999) The National Curriculum for Key Stages 1 and 2: Handbook for primary teachers in England.
(2000a) Schemes of Work for Music.
(2000b) Curriculum Guidance for the Foundation Stage.

Chapter 7

Art: 'Swirly. It's all swirly!'

Andrea Brook

'Swirly! It's all swirly!' called out a three-year-old as she painted freely in response to the African music. We were listening to a song from a CD by popular singer Oliver Mtukudzi, sent to me by a friend who was teaching in Africa. I chose the track for its variety of rhythms, and the excited child was one member of a nursery class beginning the topic of Africa. Her cries of delight came as she was responding to the African music, brushing hot paints – reds, yellows, oranges – onto a large sheet of buff paper.

NURSERY

The nursery day was organized so that the children could choose the order of their classroom activities – the art table being one of the choices. The fact that the theme was 'Africa' did not at first appear to mean a great deal to these young children, although the teachers had created an Africa room for them to explore and where they were able to carry out role-play activities. The children had also had the chance to taste African fruits and make paintings based on them.

The painting and collage activities which they undertook while listening to the African music were simply extensions of experiences the children had enjoyed – from food preparation to drama – built around the Africa topic by their teachers and other visitors to the class. Some children finished relatively quickly; others stayed with their mark-making for long periods. They showed some understanding of the link between Africa, the music and their art, asking me, 'Are you an African?' Some children were making marks in response to the rhythm by moving an inked roller in time to the music, while others added dots to their paper in response to the faster beat. However, the materials were the main concern of the children; the theme on which the activities were based played a very minor role! They had a variety of brushes, sponges and ink rollers from which to choose, but mostly they just simply enjoyed manipulating the paint.

A week later, when all the groups had worked with collage materials, the teachers' input had enabled some of the children to make closer links with the Africa theme. Comments such as 'I'm making an Africa town' were more frequent. The children were presented with a variety of hot-coloured papers and fabrics, some of which they needed to cut to a usable size while others were already small enough to use. (They particularly enjoyed the PVA glue to which food dye had been added to make a fascinating red and which many of them chose to use as paint!) As was expected their approaches were varied and the main satisfaction again appeared to come from the manipulation of the materials. Once more they were seduced by the experiences of using the materials and enjoying their different qualities.

RECEPTION

The children had begun the morning by listening to the African music as they sat on the carpet, and by making movements with their hands and arms in response to the different beats. Some responded to the slow, heavy beat, others to the faster sounds, and they were asked to imagine that they were making brush marks on large sheets of paper, with the music to inform the sorts of marks they might make. Naturally, some were more hesitant than others, and needed time to feel comfortable enough to respond openly in front of me (a stranger); others joined in the activity without reserve. We looked together at a book of photographs of African textiles and body decoration, and talked about the patterns they could see in the photographs – lots of lines and dots, and more intricate geometric designs – as well as examples of the colours they would be using in their own art work.

This was the warm-up to two of the art sessions the children were to have, based on the Africa theme chosen by the school. Using the theme both as a vehicle for the teaching of art and as a link with other areas of the curriculum seemed the way forward so that it became a part of their whole experience of Africa.

The important part of the sessions was the opportunity the children would be given to involve themselves creatively with a variety of materials using music as the chief stimulus. Since they would have the chance of working with an African drummer during the project, this seemed a valid way of linking their experiences. As teachers we were hoping they would also learn something of Africa and so broaden their understanding of the world.

The music was played once more, and the children listened to it again for a few seconds before beginning their own patterns with the paint, reacting to the rhythms and beat of the music. The art area was set out with paper and paints, and with the CD player nearby. We had chosen the hot colours of Africa, hoping they might relate them to their understanding of a different climate and way of life. By working on the buff paper, they would perhaps begin to see how powerful the colours could be.

As with the previous whole-class discussion, the differences in the children's personalities were revealed in their reactions to a number of things: the paint, the music and each other's work. Some swayed to the music as they painted; some made long and wavy marks, while others worked with dots. Some children looked around the table to see how their friends were responding to the music, and felt safe working in the same way. Each decided when his or her own painting was finished and took it proudly out into the playground to dry in the sun.

Their second session, a week later, was planned in the same way, with the children working in groups to the accompaniment of the same piece of music. Most recognized it immediately (as did their teachers), after many plays and replays! This time the class was working with printing materials and white paper. The children had sponge pieces and more rigid shapes of plastic (triangles, circles, squares and hexagons) which they used as printing blocks. They dipped them into the thick paint in the containers on the table. Most children took longer with this piece of work and became very involved with the patterns they were making. Some even dabbed their fingers into the paint, and one boy cried out in excitement, 'I'm swimming in my picture; I'm paddling in it!' The results were even more varied than the work of the previous week, with some children covering the whole sheet of paper with their marks, others using much less. Once more they worked until they felt they had completed their work – which for one or two meant most of the day!

The children needed time, but few needed support with their materials since art was a regular part of their daily curriculum. The experience of using the materials was exciting for them, however, and each approached the activities in his or her own way. One child worked slowly and methodically, creating thick stripes of different colours with the sponges; she printed on top of these to make a very textile-like piece of work, and required neither help nor encouragement from anyone, simply the time to complete the piece to her own personal satisfaction. Other children found that mixing the colours on their paper was sufficient; they delighted in the different effects they had achieved and soon felt satisfied with their work. In this way the class had been given materials to use and the opportunity to develop their skills and responses by using them in an open-ended situation.

Activities such as painting, and printing would be visited again and again during their time in reception. The materials might vary slightly, the initial stimulus differ, but the children would be encouraged to bring their own ways of responding while at the same time developing the confidence and skills to use materials freely, knowing that their work would be respected by their teachers and peers.

YEAR 1

In the Year 1 class, the children were initially given a wider choice of materials, but they had the same stimulus and opportunities to discuss the African music as a whole class, and enjoy the rhythms, patterns and colours. Materials for both printing and painting were set out together on their tables, and they too worked in groups. They then had the opportunity to choose which materials to use and how to incorporate these into their design, building on their previous experience of using them. Some chose to use both printing and painting materials for their work, while others stayed with one process.

They became very involved with the marks they were making and worked in ways that were even more varied than those of the younger children. They appeared to respond to the music, discussing the kinds of designs they were planning to make. Some complained if they were unable to hear the CD clearly, but as their designs progressed many appeared to forget about the music as they became involved with the marks and patterns they were making.

YEAR 2

In the case of the Year 2 children, the concept of Africa appeared more meaningful. One child had visited Africa, another knew someone who had been there, and they had already learned something about the continent. In their initial discussion they were able to share their perceptions and respond to the photographs showing African colours and patterns. They were working as a whole class, and their first activity was to listen to the music and try out marks on a piece of paper, using paints and different-sized brushes, to discover ways in which they could respond to the sounds. They seemed astonished at both their own work and that of their peers. Following a discussion of their first piece, they began work on a second, this time feeling more confident about the variety of marks they would be able to make – and once more they felt pleased with themselves and their differing results. Children who often held back in class were able to show their responses and received positive comments from their teacher and peers; no one appeared to feel inhibited about sharing results.

The second session involved creating simple relief-printing blocks on small pieces of card, and using their earlier work as a background upon which to print. The children looked at further examples of African designs and colours, at pictures of geometric designs on houses, and then planned and constructed their own blocks. To do this they cut out strips of adhesive draught excluder which they stuck on to small pieces of thick card. They then used black paint as a contrast to print over their initial brightly coloured paintings. They used either their first, practice, sheet or their second design, with some choosing to use each other's blocks to extend their designs. At the end of the session they sat together to talk about their work. Since they had been working as a whole class their teacher had been able to enjoy the experience with them, and her enthusiasm and excitement about their work was obviously a very positive part of the experience. She made clear that all their responses were valid, and this helped give them confidence in the use of the materials.

DISCUSSION

The activities I have described are some examples of the ways in which art can be a part of children's learning. Through engaging with the materials the children had certainly learned more about them and the different ways of using them; they had learned about themselves and the sorts of marks they (and their peers) liked to make; and they had learned something about a world beyond their own, a world they might connect with.

These sorts of experiences are precisely those which practitioners are encouraged to use with Foundation Stage children – and which lead on so smoothly to similar activities carried out at Key Stage 1. The materials had been drawn from a variety of cultures; the experiences gave the children the chance to express their ideas through a wide range of types of representation; they had time to explore and develop ideas and finish working on their ideas – as recommended by the Foundation Stage documents. There will always be opportunities to extend the children's vocabulary, whether art-related or topic-related, and the confidence they gained through working with their ideas in their own way can easily expand into other areas of their development. These sorts of experiences can be extended and built upon during Key Stage 1: the explorations and investigations, and the use of various materials along with the opportunity to develop their work and discuss it. Once more, there is the opportunity to develop vocabulary pertinent to their art work, as well as their initial ideas.

If children learn about their world through their own experiences, then the teacher has a responsibility to provide a rich range of activities to facilitate this learning. For young children this should involve plenty of first-hand exploration to encourage observation as well as help them develop sensitivity to their world and their rapidly expanding understanding of it. The art experiences we plan will require careful consideration, to allow for a variety of responses. They should excite and challenge. Preparation for art takes time and thought, but it need not be a closed activity with a defined end product in sight. At all ages, but more especially with young children, the outcomes should be determined by their own responses. This frees both children and teacher from the impossible stress of creating a set end product that can provoke frustration for some and indifference for others. This approach is consistent with the curriculum documents, but it does not imply that the teaching of art is without substance or content. The more interesting and stimulating the experiences, the more likely it is that children will want to extend their work and responses.

The approach also links with early childhood education in the north of Italy, in Reggio Emilia, where the development of extraordinary pre-schools has led educators across the world to a close examination of the approaches to education taken by the teachers. Within the schools there is an emphasis placed on the children's art education. Each school has an art teacher and an atelier where the pupils can choose to spend time working with different materials, and they are allowed to make decisions concerning their own activities and materials. They will often spend long periods working through their ideas, observed and supported (as necessary) by the art teacher. The emphasis is placed on the pupils' first-hand experiences, and art is described as one of the languages of school children – a particularly important means of expression for those who are not yet reading or writing. Art is considered one of the ways in which children learn, one of the expressions they can give to their growing understanding of the planned school experiences. This approach is not new in child education, although the emphasis on the arts is not so often seen these days. However, this approach links well with the guidance for the teaching of both Foundation Stage and Key Stage 1 children; both encourage close observation, experimentation and the discussion of ideas.

Because I was fortunate enough to spend time visiting the Reggio Emilia schools several years ago, I was able to observe young children involved in their artwork – and to see how art linked so meaningfully with all the learning which took place within the schools. I am sure that the atelier or workshop model within the classroom is one which would fit comfortably and productively with our own curriculum guidelines.

But with such apparently unstructured approaches to the teaching of art and design, how might teachers assess the children's progress? How can they know if the children are progressing through their use of the chosen materials and stimuli? As with all subjects, the assessment must be a part of the planning stage, and the aims and objectives must be included. For instance, if the teacher has planned that the children will be able to discuss their work, then time must be made available for that teacher to listen to them; if working with confidence or using materials with thought and sensitivity are aims, then the teacher will need to have opportunities to recognize and observe these attitudes and skills. The education of children in art and design will share many objectives with children's education in general, and the teacher will need to isolate both the generic aims, such as attitudes, and the more discrete aims, such as the handling of tools and increased skill with using them. The National Curriculum gives some guidelines and an overview of the expected attainment. These encourage a broad approach to art and design, linking it to the development of ideas and decision-making. This can then be seen to fit with the above methods of teaching the subject; the teacher and school can discuss the overall aims and decide how they are to be achieved.

The ideas included in this chapter could easily be fitted into any school setting, either as a part of an Africa topic or as a way of linking art and music. The African music might be one of several types of music to which the children are encouraged to respond. Alternatively, different art materials might be used: paints to allow for a fluid interpretation, plus inks with sticks and brushes, as well as charcoal or soft pastels. Encouraging children to work on to their first pieces – perhaps using charcoal or pastels on top of painted sheets –could also help them to think about the marks they have already made, and how they might extend their work.

The Africa topic was one way of extending their knowledge and perceptions of the world. However, the way it was approached and the overall experiences of the children were as important as the choice of topic, for although some of them produced stunning pieces of art work, the main value seemed to lie in the experiences themselves.

As art educator Viktor Lowenfeld wrote, back in 1947: 'For children, art is a way of learning and not something to be learned.' His approach fits that of the Italian pre-schools in Reggio Emilia – and isn't this still true for young children in the twenty-first century?

IDEAS FOR FURTHER WORK

Using the activities as starting points, work might be developed in a variety of ways: for instance, younger children might combine the collage and the printing to make joint pieces using both processes in response to the music. They might listen to more African music and make marks with feathers or sticks to represent sounds or rhythms, and create art pieces from these. The studies of patterns in African textiles could lead to some weaving, using candles to separate the dyes. Children could use the patterns on houses in Southern Africa as a basis for designing their own symmetrical patterns, printing them on to paper or model houses.

SUGGESTIONS FOR FURTHER READING

Experiencing Reggio Emilia (Abbott and Nutbrown, 2001) contains chapters by a number of educators who have been influenced by the Italian schools, and gives thoughts on specific issues in Early Years education.

Creative and Mental Growth (Lowenfeld and Brittain, 1947) still holds relevance for teachers today, helping to clarify the stages of creative growth through which most children pass, and suggesting approaches to facilitate the development of children through these stages.

BIBLIOGRAPHY

Abbott, L. and Nutbrown, C. (eds) (2001) *Experiencing Reggio Emilia: Implications for Pre-school Provision*, Buckingham: Open University Press.

Blauer, Ettagale (1999) *African Elegance*, London: New Holland Publishers.

Lowenfeld, Viktor and Brittain, Lambert (1947) *Creative and Mental Growth*, London: Collier Macmillan.

Chapter 8

Finding a voice: drama and young children

Nigel Toye

> In drama you can't talk to the participants with the status attitude like teachers talk to children. You've got to use a language code of choice, and an amount of elaboration in the language that makes them feel like they know what they're doing.
>
> (Dorothy Heathcote, quoted in Warren 1999: 29)

WHAT IS DRAMA?

It is important to understand the nature of the drama activity under discussion here. It is not a play, performance or theatre in the normal sense. Neither is it dramatic playing by children in a theme or role-play area, the commonest application of drama in the Early Years. We are concerned with a structured drama in which a teacher participates using role. It is an application of drama to classroom learning often known as 'process drama' and used for the exploration of issues and ideas:

> An active, fictional approach to learning where teacher and pupils use role and other techniques of the art form to examine key elements of a story. The fictional exploration focuses learning, with reflection in and out of role as a vital ingredient of that learning process.
>
> (Toye and Prendeville 2000: 248)

Moving 'out of role' is just as important as using role; the two go together. It gives time for the children to interpret what is happening and reflect on what to do. The reception teacher in this study noted how going out of role was 'necessary – and the children seem to accept it with no problem'. The nursery teacher observed, 'They are quite different when you're in role and when you're out of role.' She noted that 'they were more passive when I was in role whereas out of role they began talking immediately to me about what was going on'. The reception teacher agreed, commenting, when looking at the video of the nursery class, that 'going out of role to check on understanding and allow comments is even more necessary in the nursery'.

Drama is suitable for working with even the youngest children because it is based on their own pretend play, sociodramatic play:

> Early childhood educators recognise the importance of play in the education of children, but may be less likely to realise that it can lead to planned drama experiences which can extend children's knowledge and understanding.
>
> (Warren 1999: 3)

The study described here developed out of my research in a nursery school in the previous year exploring the applicability of such teacher-led (teacher-in-role) 'planned drama experiences' with three- and four-year-old children.

OUR QUESTION

We wanted to find out how children from nursery to Year 2 would respond to the same drama, with the teacher in role. Previous experience suggested to me that it would be possible, with the right choice of material, to apply the same drama across the three-to-seven-year age range. There might need to be some changes in the delivery of the material, but as drama differentiates by outcomes rather than by input the same drama might work at the different levels. We wanted to test this idea and see what different outcomes might result.

The children are able to rise to the demand because drama works on the basis that children are capable of achieving more than might be expected when working with an adult or able peers. Vygotsky terms this phenomenon the zone of proximal development:

> the distance between the actual developmental level as determined by independent problem solving and the level of potential development as determined through problem solving under adult guidance or in collaboration with more capable peers.
>
> (Vygotsky 1978: 86)

The teacher using role is a key to how drama can work across the age groups. The work is negotiated at the cutting edge of the learning. It is not the usual classroom situation where the teacher gives a series of tasks and, as the expert, waits for the children to make sense of them or ask for help. The tasks are negotiated as they are carried out because they are about dealing with the role the teacher is playing; the children are involved in a dialogue rather than in question and answer. The teacher can interact with the children, modelling commitment to the fiction and challenging their thinking from within it.

Foundation Stage children do not often meet teacher-led dramas. They tend to be catered for by the use of the home, theme, or role-play area. In my experience, much is claimed for this form of self-directed play that is not justified by the evidence. A nursery teacher with whom I was working found this to be true. When she observed children in her home corner she saw repetitive play and a very narrow range of activities. These activities contributed little to their imaginative development and provided no challenge for them, no real role play as such. It was mostly carried out solo, so she observed that 'nothing really dynamic happened'.

THE OBJECTIVES

- To plan and try out a new drama with children from each age group, nursery to Year 2.
- To collect data on the responses of the children to the drama in order to categorize similarities and differences in the responses.
- To draw conclusions as to the relative applicability of the material to each age group.

THE DRAMA

Traditional stories can be powerful bases for drama. They contain key human problems and dilemmas in powerful form, as can be seen in the objectives described below.

When I discovered that the theme for the studies in this project was Africa, I decided to look at a number of traditional African stories. I chose 'Nnenna and her Udara Tree' from *Isimeme's Stories* by Isimeme Ibazebo, one of three traditional stories from Nigeria. This story concerns a young girl whose father remarries and whose new stepmother treats her badly, making her work very hard and not giving her what she gives to her own children, a story very reminiscent of Cinderella in the Western European tradition. The key is the similarity of this story to stories the children already know and their previous experiences of adult–child relationships and problems.

The objectives of the drama

I decided to focus on key personal and social skills, one of drama's main contributions to learning for young children. The story throws up issues of fairness, parent–child relationships, dealing with an adult when your are a child, ownership, revenge and helping other people who are in trouble. These issues became the focus of the work.

To achieve the objectives, the children's role was framed as follows. The children befriend Nnenna and then discover the problem she faces with her stepmother. They are caught between the adult and child and have to sort out a reversal of power when Nnenna finally takes revenge on her step-mother and treats her badly. Dorothy Heathcote indicates how drama works by involving the children in such a problem:

> Taking a moment in time, it uses the experiences of the participants, forcing them to confront their own actions and decisions and to go forward to a believable outcome in which they can gain satisfaction.
>
> (Heathcote 1984: 99)

The roles in the drama

I used three roles, Nnenna (the girl), Mrs Ezelu (the stepmother), plus a character who does not appear in the story, a young son of Mrs Ezelu's to whom I gave the name Onye, taken from another Ibazebo story. The children were put into role as people who were very good at doing housework and helping people. This gave the children some expertise and united them so that they could explore the issues and ideas from the same viewpoint.

The stages of the drama

Each class was taken through the same drama, but in the case of the Foundation Stage children this took place in three half-hour sessions. Both Year 1 and Year 2 experienced it all in one session of just over an hour.

Part 1

Onye asked the children to help his sister, who was very grumpy because of the many jobs she had to do. The children helped Nnenna with the jobs and learned how to hide away whenever Mrs Ezelu appeared.

Part 2

The children helped Nnenna again and hid away from Mrs Ezelu, who not only treated Nnenna badly but refused to share some Udara fruit with her. Onye later shared some of his fruit.

Part 3

A week later Nnenna told them the story of the Udara tree and how this tree, grown by her from Udara seed, got bigger every time she sang to it. Mrs Ezelu discovered the tree and climbed it for the fruit. Nnenna exacted her revenge by singing the tree higher and higher before striding off and leaving her. The children had to sort out the problem, with Mrs Ezelu begging for help.

The single-session version telescoped parts one and two. Apart from this, the four dramas were essentially the same and focused on the same learning areas.

The approach and methods

The story itself was not read to the children before the drama – with the exception of one class where this happened by mistake. There was much more to the handling of the drama than this summary suggests, particularly the interchanging of roles when I was teaching it solo. I used simple role signifiers that I could pick up or put down to show when I was in and out of role. These were each of African origin and chosen to symbolize the nature of the role. It was also one of two ways of indicating the cultural difference of the story, the other being the African names. The signifiers were:

> Onye: a home-made toy motorbike, made out of tin cans.
> Nnenna: a broom, superseded by a doll when she's refusing to work any more.
> Mrs Ezelu: a reed basket.

To differentiate the task for the older children of Year 2, I adapted the household tasks and used subgroups. I also extended tasks, encouraging them to think carefully about elaborating the mime, so that polishing, for example, entailed the removal of objects, dusting, adding polish and so on. I think these extensions of an activity can often be used to differentiate for an older group.

OUR SOURCES OF INFORMATION

Data were collected in the form of my field notes, observations by the class teachers and video recordings of the sessions. In addition I held discussions with the reception and nursery teachers as they watched their own class videos and those of the other classes. Feedback from the nursery and reception children came in the form of conversations with their teachers and pictures they drew. Drama can lead to many other tasks such as speaking, writing and drawing, which are the more effective because they are contextualized.

Small groups of children from Year 1 and 2 were interviewed by a colleague not involved in the drama; the interviews were videotaped and observed by me. The videotaping went well, apart from the fact that I was unable to videotape the Year 2 session, where I was reliant on notes from observations and interviews. The children seemed to adjust easily to the presence of the camera.

WHAT WE FOUND OUT

Vygotsky: Children find a voice

I noticed that in each class the children were learning from an able peer in just the way Vygotsky predicts with his theory of the zone of proximal development (see p. 107). In the nursery group, one mature girl, Elizabeth, was influential in tackling Mrs Ezelu, the role taken by her teacher, and said how nasty she was. Asked what she looked like, she said, 'Like Mrs B. pretending', a very sophisticated reply, acknowledging both the reality and the fiction. In confronting Mrs Ezelu's unfairness to Nnenna, she modelled her feelings non-verbally as well as in words. Her teacher noted her aggressive body language, her finger-pointing, her very confident stance with defiant crossed arms. Elizabeth instructed Nnenna, 'You can tell her she can do all the jobs.' She reinforced the African context when she said she knew how to grind maize. The class followed her example and did a good job of teaching Nnenna how to use a pestle and mortar.

In the reception class, some children took the lead and showed great initiative, modelling for and enabling other children to succeed. One girl, Alice, was very proactive from early on. She led in suggesting they could tackle Mrs Ezelu if they 'dressed as adults', an intriguing idea implying that children are unable to tackle adults directly and need to become adults to do it. When I asked them to tackle Mrs Ezelu, Alice pointed out: 'We're not dressed up.' Alan developed the idea further, suggesting they were dressing 'as Mrs Ezelu's friends' and Alice added, 'Let's pretend it's a party.' All the children took up this suggestion and crowded round Mrs Ezelu to give her presents.

As other children gained in confidence their teacher saw how they were now speaking easily as though by compulsion: 'They had to say it, even though it was a secret.' Another child, Charlie, came up with a way to get Mrs Ezelu down by reversing the 'Grow, grow, grow' song, an idea which features in the story but which he had not known about. They were all very positive in tackling Mrs Ezelu on her descent: 'Apologize to Nnenna for making her do all the jobs.' Finally Charlie, who had thought of the song, also offered the means of resolving the conflict: that he could 'grow one [a second tree] for you.' Charlie was described by the teacher as being a not particularly powerful character in the class.

It might seem from the above that drama is the realm of the more able children and that the less able get something out of it as followers. To see a demonstration of the opposite of this, we only need look at the Year 1 session where it was the children with learning difficulties who were leading. Their class teacher observed that, by contrast, two of the more able girls had taken a back seat. Drama clearly provides non-verbal support for children with language difficulties and helps them find a voice. Their teachers were certainly surprised by and pleased with their contributions.

Geraldine and Sally, two of the five children in the class with special needs, were prominent. The video recording shows them as either contributing or very noticeable on sixteen occasions. I had been warned that Sally would not follow what was going on; contrary to that, she began to interact with me from a very early stage, sometimes struggling with language but always showing understanding. Later she tackled Nnenna for stranding Mrs Ezelu in the tree. 'You have to get a ladder. Then you can get her down.' It was Sally who pointed out to me, as we finished, that Mrs Ezelu had not apologized to Nnenna. I was able to remedy that omission.

Geraldine, a girl with physical and learning difficulties, wanted Mrs Ezelu to enter immediately we had organized how to hide from her. This was early on in the drama and showed she had understood the dramatic potential of Mrs Ezelu's arrival. When the children approached Nnenna's house, I noticed Geraldine, at the back of the class, mime knocking on the door. I asked her to come forward and knock for all of them. At the end it was she who told Mrs Ezelu to be 'a bit happier' when apologizing to Nnenna.

In the interview later, Geraldine showed what the drama meant to her. She described the tree taking Mrs Ezelu 'right up to the sky' and related the punishment aspect to her own situation: 'And if my mum tells me hard work in the house, I'm going to put her on the tree and on the other tree and make it go right up to the sky.' These children worked at the communication and social skills that the curriculum guidelines stress as central to their needs:

> For pupils with learning difficulties, the key skill of communication is fundamental to participation and achievement in all curriculum areas. The key skill of communication includes:
>
> - responding to others, for example, through facial expression or gestures;
> - communicating with others, for example, expressing preferences and needs;
> - interacting with others, for example, through mutual gaze with another or joint participation;
> - communicating effectively using preferred methods of communication with different groups of people;
> - communicating for a variety of purposes, for example, expressing feelings, forming and maintaining friendships, describing or commenting.
>
> (DFEE/QCA 2001: 6)

OVERALL LEARNING

The nursery class

Overall, both the nursery teacher and I saw that the most important moments were the hiding, the secret of the tree and the way the children handled the injustice. It was also clear that they would not have coped as well if the drama had not been split into sections. The teacher was surprised that they did much better than expected, but the group of ten children had been chosen from the nursery class for their maturity and they clearly coped with the complexity of the piece for that reason. She feels that drama can assist the maturation of the youngest children, their ability to handle people and each other.

In teacher-led drama we move away from the home or theme corners, where they have real things for them to role-play with, to the demand that they pretend without real objects. In this drama, for example, they had to pretend to be hiding behind non-existent curtains, marked only by canes held by two children. Their teacher saw this as an important step in developing the imaginative skills. I observed in my field notes that they were 'learning to hide behind the imaginary hangings on the imaginary wall, which they did with very clear ideas of representing crouching and hiding, something which is getting stronger session by session'.

They showed they were able to extend their activities: for example, one of the children suggested he had to go and get water from the well as part of the washing up, thus building on the sense of the African context. This development of imaginative understanding is important. They will not easily be able to do mental maths unless they develop their imagination.

The children were clear about the central moral issues: they observed of Nnenna that 'she has to do all the jobs', and 'she does not have the fruit', and noted the unfairness of that. One way in which they differed from the older children seemed to be their inability to see the connection between Mrs Ezelu's treatment of Nnenna and Nnenna's revenge. However, this event still had an impact on them. The pictures they drew later featured Mrs Ezelu stuck in the tree. Their teacher observed from the video: 'They really understood the roles and grasped the idea of role when tackling Mrs Ezelu. . . . I thought there were too many issues but they coped. They could see the injustice of it. . . . They were very assertive.'

Their learning can be related to these early learning goals:

- have a developing awareness of their own needs, views and feelings and be sensitive to the needs, views and feelings of others;
- respond to significant experiences, showing a range of feelings when appropriate;
- form good relationships with adults and peers;

- work as part of a group or class, taking turns and sharing fairly, understanding that there need to be agreed values and codes of behaviour for groups of people, including adults and children, to work together harmoniously;
- understand what is right, what is wrong, and why.

(QCA/DFEE 1999a: 24)

David struggled. He was very wary of the drama throughout, preferring to stick to his chair. Other children encouraged him to get involved, and at times he did so but then retreated. His teacher suggested he hold one of the canes marking the curtains. Having held it once, the second time they had to hide – *he* wanted to hide!

How do the youngest children stand up to adults, even when they are in role as a child? I wrote in my notes: 'Alan and Elizabeth both told Onye that Mrs Ezelu had given Nnenna all the jobs. When I, as Onye, challenged this, the bulk of the children agreed that she didn't give Nnenna the jobs. They are clearly biddable by adults.' This unquestioning response to adults could explain part of the passivity noted in this age group. Older children are much more proactive and keener to tackle an adult.

Onye did help the younger age groups. Both the reception and nursery groups needed his pressure to urge them to seek to rescue Mrs Ezelu. Both Foundation teachers noticed how well the children responded to him, probably because he was the most like them. The older children were more prepared to tackle Mrs Ezelu and Nnenna directly. The children loved the quiet moment of Nnenna sharing her secret about having a magic tree. This is where drama is close to storytelling. This was a particularly effective moment with the other classes too.

When the nursery teacher took the role of Mrs Ezelu, we were monitoring how the children 'would accept their teacher in a less sympathetic role'. I noted: 'One girl immediately pointed out that she was "nasty". This is significant because it means she is looking at the role and not seeing the teacher.' It is clear from these examples how pivotal teacher-in-role is.

The reception class

Overall, the nursery teacher, watching the video, saw that the reception class needed less guiding to conclusions, consolidations and the taking of responsibility: for example, Charlie suggesting growing the second tree. They were capable of putting the other side of arguments.

With thirty pupils in the class there were management issues and some children remained on the edges, but when the drama took hold, particularly in the second and third sections, it worked well. This class had problems at first in accepting the mime work and teacher-in-role. The occupational mimes and songs and 'hiding' pulled in some of the more reluctant or quieter children: it is important to get them active. The teacher observed, 'The quieter ones enjoyed the activity.'

It is important to have simple support activities that can be given to the more apprehensive children. Holding the canes to represent the places to hide appealed to quieter children in all of the groups. The reception teacher commented on this in her notes: 'It was excellent to see the choice of helpers to hold the canes. Emma and Mark would have enjoyed being given a set job, and Laura was a good choice as her understanding and retelling of stories is not good.' The class seemed clear that not giving Nnenna the fruit was unfair. John called it 'naughty manners'.

They responded to the demands on listening and the positive nature of the challenges. Importantly, the quieter ones were perceived by their teacher as taking in what was going on even if they were not contributing directly. Her conversations with three groups after Part 2 showed that. The three interview groups were of differing ability: below average, average, above average. She described the first group as 'three girls who had been sitting to the side together and appear to take limited involvement in the session'. The teacher noted they had to be 'drawn into discussion with questions. Their ideas did not flow.'

The second group 'had attempted to interact during the session'. Their responses elaborated on the original questions. They were described as talking 'freely about what had happened'. The third group were 'more able pupils who were *not* leaders in the session'. Their conversation was described as having 'just flowed with very little intervention or prompting from a teacher. They talked confidently.' In their pictures after the sessions most drew Mrs Ezelu and the tree, sometimes with fruit on it. One boy saw it as a beanstalk, which indicates that he was making a connection with Jack and the Beanstalk.

The Year I class

In the drama the Year 1 children initiated more ideas: for example, two boys offered to get Nnenna the fruit when her stepmother had refused her any. Three stages of thinking are demonstrated by the four Year 1 children in the interview after the drama. From initial disjointed memories they edged towards a more organized and coherent retelling of the story, which in turn led them to fill in what they felt about the broader issues. Thus originally the children offered, 'We were hiding and then Nnenna was coming', followed by 'Then we got some fruit', moving later to picking up the story-line more coherently from each other. Then, when dealing with what they felt about Mrs Ezelu being stuck up the tree, one child said 'She was very, very scared' and another, unbidden, countered: 'But it was fair because she wouldn't let Nnenna have any fruit.'

Were the mimes and singing of 'Twinkle, twinkle' too young for this group? I thought so in the session, but I may have been wrong because they burst spontaneously into the 'Grow, grow, grow' song in the interview and said how much fun it had been. The teacher was impressed by the amount of detail they remembered three and a half weeks after the drama. They were clear about the events and the morality of the piece. She concluded: 'We see the learning that children have got from what they have done with the story, how they have developed it in their own minds after the drama has finished.'

The Year 2 class

This session brought with it an interesting extra challenge because, by accident, the children had heard the original story before performing the drama. However, I decided to proceed as though they did not know it in order to see what they did with their knowledge. This was very productive. The children used their understanding to tell Nnenna what she should do.

One of the support teachers, who saw both Year 1 and Year 2, commented on the maturity with which Year 2 adapted the story. She was impressed by the speed with which they picked up the methodology, and their ability to accept my going into role (even though it was their first drama of this sort). She also commented on the authenticity of their dialogue in the latter part of the drama, when they answered spontaneously, without having to think 'What should I say?' They were saying what they thought and felt. She saw quieter children becoming involved, not inhibited by having to speak out in a large group.

Their sense of fairness and justice was to the fore. When Mrs Ezelu first confronted them at the tree in the garden, they were very aggressive towards her, telling her that she was being horrible to Nnenna. When she moved to climb the tree, they gathered tightly around the chair that was representing it to prevent her. This confrontation was very powerful and involved most of the class verbally.

They were clearly fulfilling the National Curriculum requirements:

> To speak with confidence in a range of contexts, adapting their speech for a range of purposes and audiences . . .
> To listen, understand and respond appropriately to others . . .
> (QCA/DFEE 1999: 22)

In the post-drama interview the Year 2 children were capable of broader formulations and more expansive answers. When asked what they had done with Mr Toye, the answer was: 'We were acting out a play that was set in Africa.' Then followed a detailed chronology from the entry of the first teacher-in-role through to the growing of the Udara tree, all from one child. Some of the answers were surprising but logical takes on the situation. One child, when asked what she thought about Mrs Ezelu climbing the tree, answered, 'I think she didn't know whose it was', revealing more sympathy towards Mrs Ezelu than one might have expected, because, of course, Mrs Ezelu did *not* know whose tree it was.

They were also more capable of reflection on the drama methods being used. One child, asked what she thought of stopping and starting the drama, observed: 'It was pretty good, 'cos if we planned it all out at first, we could have forgotten it and it would have taken a bit more time, 'cos we wouldn't have known what we had already been doing.' This is a quite sophisticated sense of the process method involved and of metacognition.

CONCLUSIONS

Similarities

The responses from all the classes were very positive. Each tackled the central issue of Mrs Ezelu's mistreatment of Nnenna, calling for an apology from her and saying she should take on some of the jobs herself. The PSE objectives were applicable to each of the ages, albeit at different levels of complexity. This key moment in the drama succeeded in being emotionally charged for each of the classes, providing challenge and tension, very important ingredients of drama. The drama itself was flexible and simple enough to appeal to all of the ages, yet at the same time capable of complexity as with the problem of Nnenna's revenge.

The multicultural aspect was revealing. The children at all age levels adopted and used the African names. The other multicultural element, the role signifiers, intrigued them and yet these were sufficiently universal to work. The home-made motorbike proved very attractive to the children and provided an effective symbol for the young boy, Onye. Each class had its leaders and its less vocal members, yet in each one the pupils took on the responsibility involved in working in a group and initiated ideas, even the very youngest.

Differences

Clearly, the areas of greatest disparity between the youngest and oldest children occurred in their understanding of the issues, revealed most obviously through their use of language and their ability or otherwise to interpret what was said to them and enter fully into dialogue. Having said that, in each class we noted striking examples of younger or less able children finding a voice to challenge the unfairness they perceived in the fiction.

Older children are able to sustain a task for longer. That is why the drama worked as a single one-hour session with the Year 1 and Year 2 classes. However, I would recommend that Year 1 take two shorter sessions so that the ideas can be explored fully and the group's concentration is not taxed too far.

Nursery children should be taught in groups of about ten, which gives scope for social learning and yet is manageable. The reception class of thirty worked, but I think they would have benefited from working in two half-class groups. Most Foundation classes have at least one helper, making such an arrangement possible. Older children generally possess more social skills and are capable of dealing with larger groupings without problems arising in taking turns, and so on.

Drama is powerful and underused in schools. It demands careful preparation and the commitment of the teachers to the work. We should use it selectively, but it rewards us with the liberation of both teacher and taught from their usual expectations of each other. It energizes the learning process.

IDEAS FOR FURTHER WORK

Drama and the need for speaking and listening in the Foundation Stage

For the promotion of speaking and listening in the Foundation classes the nursery teachers distinguished three different types of role play, to be employed progressively through the year: home corner, theme corner and teacher-led (teacher-in-role) drama. The home corner, a recognizable comfort zone, helps the children settle early in the year. The theme corner promotes and links the curriculum work. The teacher-led dramas provide the key opportunity for larger group work on ethical and moral issues for the children. For PSE work in as large a group as ten the teacher-led drama is essential to learning at Foundation level.

In all role play the intervention of an adult is important. The reception teacher's account of what the children were doing with their theme corner supports this. They were developing input from the adult helper who modelled use of the area for the children; for example, in 'The Travel Agent' she took on the role of a staff trainer to show the children what to do. They also had Year 4 children who came on Friday afternoons to interact with the reception children in role in the role-play area. Ideally, all classes should have teacher-led dramas.

The use of role in literacy work

Use drama in the teaching of literacy, beginning with simple hot-seating, where the teacher takes a role as someone from a story being read and/or studied, for whom the class prepare questions. This idea will work well with most age groups. The teacher has to plan the role. This does not involve acting, and should be handled as an extension of oneself but with a particular attitude. For example, taking the role of the mother or father of Max in

Sendak's *Where the Wild Things Are*: they are unhappy with Max's behaviour and want some advice on how to deal with him. Or the caterpillar in *The Very Hungry Caterpillar* by Eric Carle, who is at pains to deny that he has eaten anything or done any damage at all. For more on the use of drama in the classroom, see the book list below.

RECOMMENDED READING

Booth, D. (1994) *Story Drama*, Toronto: Pembroke Publishing.
    An interesting and thoughtful account of the process of using stories for drama.
Toye, N. and Prendeville, F. (2000) *Drama and Traditional Story for the Early Years*, London: RoutledgeFalmer.
    A detailed account of using teacher-in-role with young children, including plenty of usable full examples and beginnings of dramas.
Warren, K. (1999) *Hooked on Drama: The Theory and Practice of Drama in Early Childhood* (2nd edn), Katoomba, New South Wales: Social Science Press.
    A useful account of theory with practical examples for Early Years drama.
Winston, J. and Tandy, M. (1998) *Beginning Drama 4–11*, London, David Fulton.
    Some useful dramas and ways of approaching drama.
Woolland, B. (1993) *The Teaching of Drama in the Primary School*, London: Longman.
    A good summary of theory and practice with examples and a chapter on Key Stage 1 drama.

BIBLIOGRAPHY

Carle, E. (2000) *The Very Hungry Caterpillar*, London: Hamish Hamilton.
Ibazebo, I. (1993) *Isimeme's Stories*, Barnstaple, Devon: Spindlewood.
Heathcote, Dorothy (1984) *Dorothy Heathcote: Collected Writings on Drama and Education*, ed. C. O'Neill and L. Johnson, London: Hutchinson.
QCA/DfEE (1999a) *Early Learning Goals*, London: QCA.
QCA/DfEE (1999b) *The National Curriculum of England: English*, London: QCA.
QCA (2000) *Planning, teaching and assessing the curriculum for pupils with learning difficulties: Developing Skills*, London: QCA.
Sendak, M. (1992) *Where the Wild Things Are*, London: Picture Lions.
Toye, N. and Prendiville, F. (2000) *Drama and Traditional Story for the Early Years*, London: RoutledgeFalmer.
Vygotsky, L.S. (1978) *Mind in Society*, Cambridge, MA: MIT Press.
Warren, K. (1999) *Hooked on Drama: The Theory and Practice of Drama in Early Childhood* (2nd edn), Katoomba, NSW: Social Science Press.

ACKNOWLEDGEMENTS

Special thanks to Spindlewood Press for permission to use the story 'Nnenna and her Udara Tree' and to Chris Rowley and the Centre for Development Education at St Martin's College for advice and materials to use in the drama.

Chapter 9

The young shall inherit the technology

Pete Saunders and Liz Elliott

At the start of the twenty-first century there is a clear expectation on the part of the governments of developed countries that children will use information and communication technology in both their education and their future adult careers. For those children at the beginning of their education, ICT is included in many early years curricula. The expectations of teaching and using information technology with children under the age of eight are strongly evident. There are many areas where ICT can play a part in early years education, as suggested in the BECTA publication *Early Years Education and ICT* (2000); the authors list some common applications which range from using play telephones and programmable toys to real fax machines and cassette recorders. Many young children have already used these items before they enter school. It is perhaps in this age group more than at any other stage in the school continuum that teachers can see a definite rise, year on year, in the expectations and unconscious IT sophistication of their pupils.

In his book *Information and Communication Technology in Primary Schools* (1998) Richard Ager looks at the work of Howard Gardener and his theory of multiple intelligences. Gardener (1993) argues for eight intelligences, including the visual–spatial (thinking in images, drawing, construction) and the mathematical–logical (enjoying mathematics and science, including strategy games and experiments). Ager indicates the importance of exposing children to a broad range of stimuli and argues that with multimedia computers and information technology it is possible to use ICT to support children in learning different things in different ways. Central to any of these exploitations of computer potential are 'the abilities to navigate the electronic environment, requiring reading (and responding to) words as well as symbols, sounds and icons and also to draft, compose, refine and review text (using, for example, notes, annotations, captions, explanations, reports, reminders)'.

Well-designed software or 'intuitive user interfaces' make the first of these abilities a fairly effortless acquisition, and trial and error (trial and adjustment) invariably brings about the required result. The business of deliberate draft composition, refinements, revisits to the text, final text draft, and then further organization to 'publish' the 'ideas' is a very complex collection of synthesized intellectual and technical processes.

There exists a body of experience on the teaching of secretarial keyboard skills and the electronic preparation of commercial stationery. In recent years there has also developed a pedagogy of instruction in word processing for adults and the young literate, for the purpose of individual productivity. Word processing seems to have become an important life skill without which a person is disadvantaged in western society. More importantly, it is an arena where many refine not only the text they are composing but the very thoughts they are incubating. To wait until a person is conventionally 'literate' before allowing them the benefits of word processing seems to be a waste of a valuable opportunity.

There is, however, no body of knowledge from which we can draw lessons regarding how and when to expose very young children, whose literacy is only partially developed, to the potential of word processing. For instance, for most areas of development the balance between direction and exploration is well understood by nursery and infant teachers; this is true whether considering a strand of mathematical understanding or making biscuits. This same balance is not generally understood in the realm of word processing. Very little is known about how much and which strands of the complex word processing skills need to be taught by direction, learned as a consequence of teacher-managed experiences, games and puzzles, or developed as a result of intuitive exploration, fortunate accident or plain curiosity.

As part of an exploration into providing ICT-based 'different learning' we were interested in the use of personal computers – and, specifically, the use of word processors – by young children. Developing symbolic and written communication is an important part of a young child's early experience at school. As mentioned before, a growing number of children have access to computers at home and observe their parents and older siblings using word processors to generate text. The term 'word processing' here could mean a desktop publishing package, e-mail, web chatroom or caption-writing – quite literally, any software which processes words to enable people to communicate effectively through the medium of text. The major advantage of word processing over paper-based writing is that it allows easy drafts and multiple redrafts. These can be assisted by combinations of hardware and software, the use of conventional keyboards or alternative input devices and software support, such as vocabulary lists, word banks and spell checkers at the touch of a button, click of a mouse or key selection.

As we adopt word processing as our principal means of communicating through text, we also adopt routines and approaches which are altogether different from those associated with manuscript texts. We are able to relax about their writing, approaching it according to priority ideas, maybe not in their eventual order, maybe not with all the quotations exactly referenced or the technical terms correctly spelt; these things can be the object of later attention. The main message gets composed while the idea is 'hot'.

This marked change in adult approaches to writing does not have its parallel in the world of the three-to-sevens. In theory, these children might never need to know about the frustrating three- or four-year apprenticeship required to enable an individual to hand-write with sufficient fluency and legibility a worthy composition (or, alternatively, laboriously rewrite multiple drafts). We could ask whether by using word processors alongside the gradual development of handwriting we might increase children's understanding of the creative writing process. Such a process then becomes possible without the limitations imposed by a lack of pen control or an inability to correctly scribe punctuation, composition, spelling, pace and structure as a single act of creative synthesis. For them, word processing is not a change of approach to writing; it could be their natural writing future and no stranger than learning to avoid falling over on roller skates or picking up the rules of a new playground variant of 'chase'. This newly emerging 'electronic age citizen' is therefore a fascinating subject for educational research. Our interest lies in two areas.

OUR QUESTIONS

First of all we would like to understand more about the ways children at the emergent-writing stage take to word processing and, from that, learn more about how we can enable the most efficient development of ability, facilitate the most natural progressions and recognize which experiences are important to the development of a secure capability. Second, we would like to know if certain skills and types of knowledge are order-dependent or rely on associated knowledge and concepts. We are also aware that any short-term research is unlikely to deliver complete answers, although we hope for at least some clarification of issues which could start to inform good practice.

It is not difficult to show a direct link between pupil proficiency at operating creativity or productivity software, such as word processors, and the extent to which the children are able to exploit it to benefit their overall educational opportunities. However, it is the means by which they acquire that proficiency which seems to us a fruitful focus point. For this case study we considered the progression of pupil capability and looked for a continuous development where:

- exploration, experiment, exercises and tasks each played their parts, along with
- instruction, direction and challenge;
- demonstration, exposition and consolidation;
- and well-placed review, reflection and evaluation.

A number of subskills are involved in developing a piece of text, whether an abstract pattern of letters and symbols or an evocative poem. These skills may be conveniently classified as operational, intellectual or literary.

We decided to undertake a case study which looked at children's use of word processing from a very young age in a nursery school (3–4 years) progressing through the use of the same technology in a reception class (4–5 years), a Year 1 class (5–6 years) and finally two Year 2 classes (6–7 years). Although we had a planned structure for the pupil activities, this was still an action research study, as we were prepared to adjust the structure to suit the circumstances and pedagogic decisions in the light of observations of the children with whom we were working.

Our work in the schools

We worked with one group of children who attended a morning session each week at Brantwood Nursery School and three age groups from reception to Year 2 at Clappersgate Primary School. At Brantwood Nursery we looked at using a basic word processor and standard keyboard to explore simple pattern-making using letters based on those in the child's own name. This provided some interesting pointers for later research but also served as a useful orientation exercise and informed our preparations for working with the Key Stage 1 children.

At Clappersgate Primary, we followed a single theme across the three age groups based on the act of 'retelling a story'. We introduced each of the classes to the same African fable about an unpleasant boy who turned into an ugly cat and eventually learned about caring for and understanding others. We asked the children to retell this story.

In order to select appropriate and challenging retelling modes, we researched and observed the children working, checked on the common writing software in each classroom, consulted the class teacher, and gained information and ideas from the children themselves. What emerged from this was a pattern, which gave us a model of continuity and progression to use as a reference point. These three short projects may well act as pointers to progression but they do not convey any absolute appropriateness of task for the age or year group. As clearly indicated in *Curriculum Matters 15* (HMI 1989) the work which is appropriate is that which builds on the competence already achieved, regardless of the age of the pupil.

Furthermore, in spite of modern educational structures which attempt to ascribe particular capability to a particular age, we must be aware that literally every year primary teachers are faced with new classes which are more IT-sophisticated that the previous ones. In some schools this phenomenon may already be very marked, which calls for continual adjustment in the presentation of classroom resources and constant refinement of expectations.

What we were able to achieve in our brief classroom research opportunity was a pattern or model of development in operational, intellectual and literacy skills which appears to have been engaging and rewarding for the pupils. This served as a useful start to the more in-depth study of what enables the development of proficiency and whether there is a particular order of subskills acquisition that is the most efficient.

Brantwood Nursey School: letter patterns

At Brantwood Nursery School we observed closely the free-will activities of children who elected to 'work' on the computer, who were used to response software (it does something and the child responds) and who were now confronted with a content-free environment (it does not 'do' anything). In this instance we had set up MS Word with a pre-selected, appropriate font size and style. The suggestion to children who elected to investigate this work choice was that they might each make a pattern of the initial letter of their name. Usually this simply triggered a series of explorations, with some children being quite adventurous and others making only modest sorties into the realms of 'cause and effect'. Consequently one pupil became active in changing font size and colour, adjusting margins and filling pages of repeated characters, while another was apparently satisfied with the repeated use of the spacebar, a single character key and the backspace/delete key. During these five morning sessions it became evident that, regardless of the depth of engagement, there was a fairly constant attention span of about twelve minutes. There was no problem at all associated with upper-case keys delivering lower-case versions of the letters, and with hindsight it may even have been patronizing of us to have pre-selected a 'sensible' typeface. We were surprised by the attitude of these pre-school, as yet un-institutionalized, children to their creations. It is true that most of the children were happy or even proud to have a printout of their efforts to put in their work folder, but this was not of burning importance. Some of the children preferred to 'rub out' work and do something different. This may have been because of an impression that, like a chalkboard, it is necessary to release 'page space' in order to continue working. However, observations of children suggest to us that this was not the likely explanation. We suspect that these children are simply rewarded by the process and much less by the product. This research provided us with preparation and orientation for our Key Stage 1 study.

Clappersgate Primary School

At Clappersgate Primary School there were three stages of word processing involvement, with the children spanning a twenty-four-month age difference. There are no doubt many intermediate stages, but these worked well in this particular study. The three stages were scribing for a big book, caption-writing for a video of 'stills', and pasting sentences into hyperlinked pages.

We developed retelling opportunities targeted at the different age groups. All the children were told the story with some listener participation, as is usual for this age range. In each case there was some discussion about the oral tradition and how stories are never exactly the same when retold. We hinted that there was room for slight changes of detail, that it was unimportant if some details were omitted and that a story could sometimes be improved if extra details were added. We emphasized that their story would remain recognizably the same, even after a chain of retelling. After a few meetings we taught the children an African song, which also tells a version of the story. This enjoyable confirmation of the variety of ways it is possible to retell the 'same' story was crowned with a recording of Ladysmith Black Mambazo singers presenting 'The Boy Who Turned into a Cat', the authentic rhythms of which conveniently fitted some elementary African dance and drumming taught to the children by Raymond Otto from the Takalini Dance Theatre.

The reception class: writing a big book

For the reception class children we introduced the retelling through illustrative drawings. We told them we were going to make a book to retell the story, so it was important that they illustrated different parts of it. They were familiar with big books and easily persuaded to talk about their pictures. Each child was asked to bring his or her picture to the computer and tell one of us a sentence or phrase that should go with the picture. We each acted as a scribe, and this dialogue between scribe and 'author' proved a valuable one for the children. They were certainly very attentive and stimulated by seeing their words appear as 1cm-high characters on the screen.

We used Comic Sans typeface to avoid the non-cursive 'a'. The choice of word processor was not critical, but we used the Write On program as this was installed as standard classroom software. The big book was put together by adults with some editorial pupil involvement, and acted as a reminder of the story but also as an opportunity for the children to experience a taste of 'writing for an audience'. Here the computer (under adult control) was able to deliver text (originated by the pupil-spoken word) in the recognizable form of the big book captions. We assume that this provided a graphic contribution to children's understanding of 'how to share their ideas by presenting information in a variety of forms' (NC 2000).

Although the children in this one-to-one situation were alert and apparently assimilating a great deal of information, it remained a passive engagement as far as the computer was concerned. There would clearly come a time when there would be insufficient novelty to sustain attention without more practical involvement on the part of the children. As a next step, an adult could write their words on a slip of paper for the class to transcribe, letter by letter, on to the computer with adult supervision to assist with sorting out minor imperfections (necessary when text is for publication). This copy typing is a far cry from composing at the keyboard but is a useful step towards the acquisition of more focused operational knowledge.

Progression from that activity might include extra tasks such as clicking the resave button (if the blank document had already been saved by an adult and ascribed a filing address), the addition of author initials and clicking on the print button for a draft print.

Year 1: a video story

The work with the Year 1 children also started with the telling of the African fable about a rude boy who turned into a weird five-legged cat and suffered humiliation until he had adjusted his attitude. The children became very involved with the details of the tale and its moral issues. It was not difficult to get them to help the retelling process by 'composing at the keyboard' a single sentence that described the part of the story they wanted to illustrate. The adult in this situation was advisor/mentor and technical assistant but adopted a hands-off role with regard to the computer. Again the particular word processor for this task was irrelevant, the most suitable one being the one with which the children were most familiar. The class also created illustrations on paper with pencils and felt-tips, but it was the text that would rule the composition. In the big-book construction the story in pictures was captioned. With this retelling, the text (video captions, narration and script) would hold the story together, the illustrations taking a secondary role even though they would have visual dominance.

With all the twenty-four text contributions printed out on strips of paper, an editorial group of six pupils was set the task of ordering them. A great deal of reading aloud on the part of pupils and teacher provided a close focus for an extended span of attention, and when the order was agreed and the final rereading approved, the strips were numbered. Out of sight of the children the texts were cut and pasted into MS Word (the researcher's customary word processor, but almost any word processor would suffice) and centred, enlarged and printed on individual A4 placards. These were hand-numbered on the reverse for the performers' convenience.

Groups of four at a time came to the video recording studio (cloakroom) for the production stage. A video camera was set up on a sturdy tripod and zoomed and focused to record an A4 page placed in landscape orientation on a music stand. One at a time, according to the running order, the children placed their pictures on the stand, checked through the eyepiece that these were in frame and then on signal read their captions aloud (maybe several times to get a good, well-paced, strongly voiced performance).

The adult operated the camera but – as a development of this IT activity – subsequent progression could involve pupils operating the camera for takes and even setting up the recording desk.

After a good voice print with the camera capturing the picture, the equipment was paused and the picture replaced by the caption sheet. This was then recorded for about six seconds. The procedure was repeated for each of the contributors. A surprise during this process was the fascination the video camera held for the children. It was certainly a treat to see their pictures through the camera's eyepiece, even though the real artefact was an arm's length away. This attraction could perhaps be exploited in other IT capability developments and the recording of events, achievements and creations.

Post-production work was completed by adults so that recording from the camera to VHS domestic video recorder allowed the omission (editing out) of errors and surplus retakes. On reflection this denied the children an important link with the process, and it may have been more logical to allow them to experience the first cut, a showing of the complete unedited recording, warts and all. This could have alerted them to the need to return to the product, edit and refine it. It is possible that some of the children may have been led to imagine that the fairly straightforward process of the recording session resulted in the final product.

The product was a fine video retelling of the story. The children retold it through a composed and refined text, the voice recording of 'public speaking' and the reading and presentation of imaginative narrative illustrations. Although the children 'made' a video retelling they did not physically appear on the recording and their names were restricted to forenames only, which seemed a pragmatic security measure. Our involvement with the project and associated experiences aside, we again assume that a contribution to the children's further understanding was made, as was shown by their ability to share their ideas by presenting information in a variety of forms, and that information technology can provide combinations of solutions for the communication and broadcasting of that information.

Year 2: a story on disk for the Clappersgate web site

The Year 2 classes were introduced to the story in a similar way, and the retelling activities included the African song and picture-making. The pictures were scanned and stored as separate files; in fact, adult processing allowed the high-resolution scanned images to be reduced to screen-resolution quality with a considerable saving in disk space. We thought this process was beyond the children's comprehension, but a similar outcome could be achieved with pupil participation by capturing the pictures with a digital camera pre-set to low resolution. Recently we have had success with this type of activity using the Sony Mavica range, where a standard floppy disk is removed from the camera and inserted directly into the computer for immediate access without the need for cables or transfer software.

The text was composed at the keyboard by collaborative groups of two or three pupils. Although there was adult supervision and a little mentoring, the groups also displayed corporate editorial cooperation and a willingness to refine sentences for best reading. Typically a writing consortium produced two or three sentences and, after the file had been saved under adult supervision, the text would remain on the screen for the next group to see in order to consider their continuation sentences. This process could also have been assisted by a draft printout of all the contributions, stapled in order, as a desktop reference.

Away from the children a hyperlinked 'book' was compiled using MS Publisher, but any one of a number of other programs could be used, including Hyper-Studio, Text-Ease or PowerPoint. The book had each text file pasted in and displayed as a separate page with plenty of room for an illustration. Also on each story page was a forward and backward page-turning icon in the bottom corner. Under adult supervision, the children rejoined the activity with the explained task of accessing the store of image files, identifying their own, inserting it into the prepared frame and making such adjustments as would tidy the page.

Again the children were able to add to their appreciation of the variety of ways in which they could 'use ICT to help them generate, amend and record their work and share their ideas in different forms' (NC 2000: AT Level 2). The children were very pleased with the final result and it is ready – saved as an HTML file and viewed via a web browser – to be copied to individual pupil disks for home viewing or placing on the school web site. This is a very real case of writing for an unseen audience.

If a similar venture were to be attempted with these same children, their capacity for taking greater responsibility would be increased due to their appreciation of the linear process and the targeted outcome. Their ideas for improvements and innovations along the way would be valid and could be actively explored, either individually or as part of the corporate endeavour. The level of ICT autonomy could also be increased, with particular emphasis (since this would be a joint ownership project) on security 'backing-up' and other organizational structures such as having separate folders for text files, picture files and even sound files, plus a logical file-naming protocol.

Overall we were able to experience different approaches apparently appropriate for the three different age groups but basically consisting of the same activity: the retelling of a story with the assistance of ICT apparatus. We are confident that departures from commercially prepared 'educational' (response) software lend themselves to a far greater appreciation of the potential of ICT, provide more opportunities for learning in real contexts and a better prospect for the realization of creative potential.

Readers will have noticed that all these episodes involved ordinary class-room teaching up to the point of working at the computer; then we slipped into the one-to-one or small-group teaching mode. Two observations are worth making here. First, there are many areas of skills development, from reading to riding a bicycle, where effective learning is unlikely without some investment of one-to-one teaching. In this respect learning the operational skills of content-free software is no different, and it would be a shallow excuse to deny children such one-to-one or small-group attention on the grounds of obvious 'impossibility'. Teachers are constantly finding opportunities for one-to-one teaching, particularly in areas where they are confident. This can be a problem, of course, but it is a classroom management problem, not one associated particularly or exclusively with ICT.

The second point we want to make is that the investment of one-to-one or small-group attention will result in greater true autonomy, the gradual development of pupil control over the technology and an increase in the amount of independent work freed from constant procedural, operational or mechanical confusions, problems and upsets. The work we have undertaken with these children has demonstrated that they have truly inherited the technology, and there is an imperative to invest in their early acquisition of operational and intellectual ICT skills, particularly in the realm of processing words, in order that are not denied their birthright.

IDEAS TO TRY IN YOUR OWN SCHOOL SETTING

- Act as the computer scribe for very young children retelling a story. Sit at the computer with them while they tell you their version of the story and type in the text as they speak. You can read it back to them and check that you have got it down correctly. Remember that this is their work and you are just the scribe. The learning and teaching is in the discussion and you are presenting a word-processing role model for them.
- Use a tape recorder to record their retelling of a story or part of a story. It may be that they have drawn an illustration and you can get them to describe what is happening in the picture. This recording should then be made available for other children to listen to. You can encourage the children to develop the technical skills to make their own recordings independently.

SUGGESTED READING

Richard Ager's book *Information and Communication Technology in Primary Schools* (1998) is an interesting introduction to the subject of ICT in the primary context and contains a chapter on ICT in the Early Years.

BIBLIOGRAPHY

Ager, R. (1998) *Information and Communications Technology in Primary Schools*, London: David Fulton.

BECTA (2000) http://www.becta.org.uk/technology/infosheets/html/foundationstage.html

Gardener, H. (1993) *Frames of Mind. The Theory of Multiple Intelligence*, London: Fontana Press.

HMI (1989) *Curriculum Matters 15: Information Technology from 5–16*, London: HMSO.

Ladysmith Black Mambazo (1994) *Gift of the Tortoise* (audio CD), Warner Bros.

Chapter 10

Out of Africa? Lullabies, riddles and stories

Katharine Langley-Hamel and Kevin Hamel

We wanted to combine some elements of well-known western stories and rhymes with some broad aspects of traditional African storytelling. Riddles, songs and stories are an essential part of the instruction of children in traditional non-literate societies. Codes of behaviour, and even advice on survival, are communicated orally. We were not presuming to tell African stories in authentic ways, but by recognizing children's past experience we hoped to identify universal themes and use these as the basis for enrichment.

We chose lullabies, riddles and stories as familiar starting points for exploration. Sam Twiselton, a colleague in the English department at St Martin's who had enjoyed working with children and teachers at Clappersgate on previous projects, was keen to join us.

LULLABIES: RECEPTION

Reception children had been exploring the theme of Africa. This was reflected in the classroom: African animals peered out of jungle greenery and both fiction and non-fiction books reinforced the African theme.

Why lullaby?

We were attracted by the universal appeal of the lullaby, and its evident purpose. Lullabies are sung everywhere, yet these songs also reflect landscapes, the struggles of everyday life, and the social groups and values of a society. As well as soothing a crying child to sleep, an African lullaby has an additional and equally important function: 'at the same time, it expresses [a] mother's gratitude toward Nature – or God – for having given her a child, a privilege denied so many other women' (Beeby 1969: 6). The focus on lullaby offered opportunities for making links with the children's own experiences, and encouraging them to share them with others. They also moved from the security of their common experiences to a consideration of lullabies within other cultures.

Lullabies provide an excellent context for shared writing with young children and a basis for substitution, extension and shared composition. There are opportunities to extend vocabulary through sharing and exploring the language in a lullaby and then encouraging children to use these new words when talking about their own experiences. Consideration of shared experiences provides an excellent opportunity for children to engage in 'talk for writing', emphasized throughout the National Literacy Strategy guidance, *Developing Early Writing* (DFEE 2001). Above all this theme provided an opportunity to have fun with language.

We asked the children how they might get a fretful baby brother or sister to sleep. Suggestions included taking the baby for a walk, rocking the baby, and then Zak's observation: 'You could sing "Rock-a-Bye Baby".' This led to a discussion of lullabies: why do they help to send a baby to sleep? A number of children suggested that because these songs were quiet they settled and soothed the baby. This led to a consideration of lullabies the children already knew, most of which turned out to be their own versions of 'Rock-a-Bye Baby'.

The focus turned to lullabies in other lands, including Eastern Europe and the United States. Kevin led the singing, accompanying the children on his guitar. This led to a consideration of an African lullaby, accompanied this time by a drum. We had great fun asking the children for advice on ways in which the drum should be played; everyone agreed it should be played quietly if it was not to wake the baby. They passed it around and tried different ways of playing it: making a circular motion with the flat of the hand, scratching it with fingernails, tapping it gently with one or two fingers. Kevin combined these suggested techniques in a subsequent performance of the lullaby. This linked with the QCA guidance for music, where children are encouraged to select sounds and dynamics reflecting the mood of chants and songs.

Katharine then focused on the sounds and structures of lullabies, drawing the children's attention to the repetition, lulling language and use of alliteration. Sam demonstrated the way in which a skilled writer would write down these phrases, thinking out loud during the process. Children were then asked to talk to a partner and to consider the words and phrases that would help them to sleep. Many suggestions were forthcoming, reflecting personal experiences. These included: 'Sleep, little baby, sleep', a rather irritated 'Just be quiet and get to sleep', 'rocking', 'quietly' and 'creep'. Sam acted as scribe at this point, recording the children's words and talking to them about the decisions they had made and supporting their composing process.

We then drew their attention to the message carried by African lullabies. The children talked to their partners again about the messages that parents might sing. They quickly identified a range of phrases resulting from their own experiences. These included 'You're my special little darling', 'I love you' and 'You're my princess.' This was followed by group work in which the children produced independent writing and drew words, phrases, sentences and images conducive to sleep. Some of these were combined to produce gentle, rhythmic chants by the whole class.

The activities provided a context for valuable oral work arising from a discussion of meaningful experiences. Children were able to play with language and to enjoy manipulating sounds and rhythmic patterns. Additionally, they were presented with a motivating context for each stage of the shared writing process

The children's sensitivity to the use of loud and quiet sounds (dynamics) was enhanced through a consideration of the purpose of lullabies. Crucially, their awareness and appreciation of the similarities and differences of an aspect of another culture were awakened through moving from the familiar to the less familiar.

PARTICIPATION IN GROUP STORYTELLING: YEAR 1

Pupils in Year 1 had previously listened to stories about Africa and explored some techniques of African art. They had experimented with African motifs and patterns and been inspired by the visit of an African drummer. We wished to draw on these experiences in approaching a story set in an African context.

The focus of the session was a story called *The Hunter* by Paul Geraghty, who was born and grew up in South Africa. In the story a little girl, Jamina, accompanies her grandfather into the bush to collect honey. She hopes she might see elephants. Her grandfather tells her that elephants are seldom seen because of hunters. While playing make-believe hunting games, she wanders away and gets lost in the bush. Then Jamina hears a distressed baby elephant, orphaned by hunters. She resolves to lead the baby elephant home, in the hope of finding the remainder of the herd on the way. A storm and torrential rain impede their progress. When the rain stops, Jamina imagines she can hear elephants. But it is just the wind blowing through grass. Jamina and the elephant follow the zebra as far as the river, but are unable to cross because of the crocodiles. After a number of setbacks, the little elephant is reunited with the remainder of the herd, and Jamina falls fast asleep, to be found by her mother.

The children had particularly enjoyed *The Hunter* during their reception year, and readily contributed elements to be incorporated in a class story entitled *The Lost Elephant*. Although Paul Geraghty is a South African writer and illustrator, *The Hunter* is not a traditional African story. African storytellers rely on the participation of the audience – certain responses are expected at key points in the narrative. We thought we could adapt *The*

Hunter and introduce patterned repetitive phrases, and sung and chanted responses, to our new story. There are groups of stories which depend heavily on the listener's responses. They are frequently based on clear repetitive forms and include The Gingerbread Man, and the Three Little Pigs. As expected, the children were familiar with a number of these stories. We were able to:

- build on this shared past experience;
- revisit a familiar story, *The Hunter*;
- combine both elements to introduce a familiar structure in the context of a known story;
- introduce new expectations of their roles as listeners and storytellers.

After hearing the story again the children were asked what they thought Jamina had learned from her adventures. Almost without exception, they considered she had learned the importance of taking notice of adult advice in order to 'keep safe'. We asked the children to identify the significant incidents in which Jamina had made unwise decisions. We then talked about ways in which this could be made apparent to listeners.

The story game *Going on a Bear Hunt* is familiar to, and popular with, most children at Key Stage 1. The perception of danger (imaginary or real) is signalled by the response: 'Uh oh!' We adopted the repetitive framework of *We're Going on a Bear Hunt* for *The Lost Elephant*. Building on prior knowledge of this structure, children signalled Jamina's poor decisions (leading to real or imaginary dangers) by responding 'Uh oh!'

The singing game '*Che che kole*' was introduced. This is a 'call-and-response' game originating in Ghana. Performing this marked the journey of Jamina and the lost elephant as they travelled from one encounter to the next. In *The Lost Elephant* the song continues the narrative and provides the commentary, the words of the song changing every time it is heard. For example:

> Sun is shining, sun is shining.
> Feeling happy, feeling happy.
> Wind is blowing, wind is blowing.
> Grass is moving, grass is moving.

During an exciting session the children contributed to these chants, selecting their words carefully. The words were recorded during shared writing. The children were then asked to retell the story, elaborating on significant incidents. This formed the basis of shared writing and subsequent independent work leading to a whole-class performance in which ideas were shared and combined.

RIDDLES: YEAR 2

We used riddles as the basis of our work with Year 2 children. The origins of the riddle are lost in antiquity. Riddles offer

> veiled and interesting descriptions of the subject which provide enough information and clues without giving the answer away too easily. . . . The lines of a riddle also have a magical quality about them: something of the element of chants and spell.
>
> (Brownjohn 1994: 112)

In traditional non-literate societies, riddles are used to pass on received wisdom with elegance and wit. The finest riddles present seeming contradictions and paradoxes. The riddler's art is to intrigue and mislead the listener. As Brownjohn observes, if children are not allowed to mention a subject they are forced to call upon their powers of observation and description. Yet very young children are able to appreciate the art of the riddle, and are able to make up their own; sometimes with remarkable results. Pupils in Year 2 had been working on objectives relating to the posing of relevant questions prior to reading a non-fiction text and the use of scanning to locate specific information. They had also been introduced to the concept of riddles in line with the objectives for fiction and poetry. We decided that these objectives could be combined effectively to provide a motivating activity and consolidate learning in both areas.

During shared work the children were asked to define a riddle. This produced a range of responses, including 'a puzzle', 'a song' and 'a poem'. Sam then challenged them with a riddle and asked them to think about the way in which they solved the puzzle. They were aware of the need to reserve judgement, to avoid jumping to conclusions about the veiled hints: 'We don't know it's a dog yet; just because it's got legs and a tail, it could be anything. I'm waiting.'

Then they were asked to think about the ways in which they could use this information to help them to invent their own riddles. They were shown enlarged, illustrated, non-fiction texts about various African animals. They were asked to scan the texts and to select three or four facts that could form the basis of a riddle. Sam demonstrated the writing process and supported the children in a shared composing of a riddle before asking them to invent their own independently. They worked enthusiastically and produced riddles with varying degrees of sophistication. They all made reference to the information in the text; some used the pictures as an important source of information, observing small details with precision. Several children were very aware of the need to trick the reader: 'I'm going to say that it [a gazelle] runs very fast right at the start, so that they'll all think it's a cheetah, that will fool them.' The whole-class session was used to highlight the ritual and rhythms of words and phrases by exploring different ways of singing and chanting the riddles. This shared experience ensured that the pupils' initial perception of riddles as puzzles, songs and poems were realized.

Opportunities were provided for the class to extend their skills in locating information in non-fiction texts. They were encouraged to write with a sense of audience in mind, manipulating language, selecting words and ordering their thoughts with care. The session closed with a lively and enthusiastic group performance of chanted riddles. The children were left with a sense of achievement, an awareness of the power of language and, above all, the enjoyment of playing with language.

FOLLOW-UP IDEAS

Skills in retelling stories as a group could be extended by:

- Using props, story boards or story maps;
- Exploring settings in more detail;
- Rewriting specific incidents, with the adult demonstrating first how to do this or scribing for the group.

Work on riddles could be developed by:

- Refining scanning skills to locate specific information in non-fiction texts;
- Children using ICT to compile their own book of riddles; accessing one of the internet 'riddles' web sites;
- Developing children's sense of audience (or of readers) so that they understand the need to make up riddles requiring more complicated thought.

BIBLIOGRAPHY

Beeby, F. (1969) *African Music: A People's Art*, New York: Lawrence Hill.
Brownjohn, S. (1994) *To Rhyme or Not to Rhyme? Teaching Children to Write Poetry*, London: Hodder & Stoughton.
DFEE (2001) *The National Literacy Strategy: Developing Early Writing*, DFEE Publications.
Geraghty, P. (1994) *The Hunter*, London: Hutchinson.
Rosen, M. (1996) *We're Going on a Bear Hunt*, London: André Deutsch.

OTHER RESOURCES

'Tuned-in' primary website: *The Lost Elephant*, www.tuned-in.org

Discussing the picture

After the summer half-term break the teachers from Brantfield Nursery and Clappersgate Primary School and the college tutors met on an appropriately hot and sunny afternoon to review, celebrate and evaluate the 'Africa' project. The agenda was to address our two initial questions:

- Had the project supported the transition process from nursery to primary school?
- Had the Africa theme enhanced children's understanding of cultural diversity?

We also wanted to consider the highlights and difficulties we had encountered and to what extent the case study might inform and develop future practice.

TRANSITION FROM NURSERY TO PRIMARY SCHOOL

Veronica Boles, the teacher from Brantwood Nursery School, began by describing a high point when the nursery children had visited Clappersgate towards the end of an afternoon and observed the Year 2 children playing their African rhythm music, then been drawn in to participate themselves:

> All the parents and older children and grandparents gradually slipped in quietly to watch. If so many people had been there to start with the nursery children would have been petrified, but they came in gradually, informally, so the nursery children just carried on. Then the parents took their nursery children and the older children home together. It was a good chance for me to see the children I'd previously had in the nursery too and how they'd grown.

The whole project, Veronica said, had given the nursery teachers and the reception teacher an opportunity to 'follow things through – to see how themes could be extended, across the age range'.

Pat Spencer, the Year 2 teacher, talked about raised awareness and sharing: 'It wasn't so much that it increased my understanding of progression in children's development from three to eight – more that it gave us time to talk together and reflect on it.' Andrea Brooke, the art tutor, agreed. 'I enjoyed seeing Nigel's drama sessions across the age range on the video; the sharing was important', she said. 'It would have been nice if we could have had an art exhibition too, for children and parents to see the progression.' 'We could do that next time as part of a book week, or a writing week', Pat suggested. 'And we could invite the children's parents in to watch the videos with us. And we really must look at the story video and the music videos together. What we have done so far was not "crisp" enough for the children and parents to really see the continuum – to track things through.'

WAS AFRICA A SUITABLE THEME FOR DEVELOPING CHILDREN'S AWARENESS OF CULTURAL DIVERSITY?

'We wondered about the theme initially, but it really went down well with the nursery children', Veronica said. The nursery nurse, Jane Lambert, added that Alec's mother said that he had seen pictures of Africa on television and told his family that he 'knew all about Africa'.

It was agreed that the emphasis in the stories had been on 'mud huts and jungles, not cities', although the drama and ICT had been set up to examine similarities in child–parent relationships across those communities. 'Yes – good personal and social education', someone said. 'The dilemmas children confronted in the stories spilled into circle time and religious education.' The art and music sessions were seen as very successful and capable of much more development. It was agreed that, while the emphasis had been primarily on music, art, drama and stories in African contexts, raising children's awareness of cultural diversity was an implicit dimension. This too was capable of further development.

HIGHLIGHTS

Raymond Otto and his drumming sessions scored highly: 'Exciting stuff.' There was also agreement about how articulate children became when talking about their ideas and experiences in art, music and drama – and also in ICT – and the positive impact their excitement and success in these areas had on their self-esteem. Kirsty said that when the nursery children got talking about music she was amazed at how much they had to say, and that when she developed their discussion with Year 1 and 2 children they had 'really sophisticated ideas'. Drama, too, had 'raised the self-esteem and status within the class of children who were not academic' across the age span. Similarly in art, 'When Andrea invited children to explain their work those who excelled were not generally regarded as the most articulate, yet they often have most to say.' 'I was pushed a bit by Hilary to carry the drama through each age group', Nigel admitted, 'but I am pleased about that because at each of the levels the children taught me a lot.' The nursery and infant teachers arranged to swap their drama videos and meet with Nigel to discuss them further.

CAN THE PROJECT INFORM AND DEVELOP FUTURE PRACTICE?

Pete Saunders said he now had a lot of very positive data on emergent word processing which he would be able to share with student teachers, to help them develop their own insights. Pat Spencer felt that working with Andrea Brook had shown her how to develop QCA schemes for art in a whole new variety of exciting contexts: 'It's great to see how National Curriculum and QCA objectives can be achieved in different ways.' Other comments made were:

It's helpful to see how to make links between subjects, in this day and age.

It's good to have our awareness of creativity raised, and to see that, in spite of SATs and everything, it can have a place.

The project gave us a chance to re-evaluate what is important – to concentrate on developing the social skills and self-esteem of all children.

Teachers and tutors parted bubbling with optimism, and promises that 'we must continue to work together in this way' – but will time allow?

The college tutors probably saw the continuum more clearly because they were all involved with each age phase. It was agreed that time is the great enemy for everyone. 'We really need funding to allow us to really develop this work.'

RESOURCES REFERRED TO IN THE TEXT

The Horniman Museum and Gardens, 100 London Road, London SE23, tel: 0208 6991872, email: www.clothofgold.org.uk/inafrica

BIBLIOGRAPHY

Andreae, G. (1996) *Rumble in the Jungle*, London: Orchard.
Brown, E. (1994) *Handa's Surprise*, London: Walker Books.
McKee, D. (1989) *Elmer*, London: Andersen Press.

Part 3

Market Gates Infants' School and St Mark's day care unit pre-school playgroup

Our environment – history, geography and physical education

Table 3.1 Playgroup outline plan for 'Our environment' showing links to areas of learning

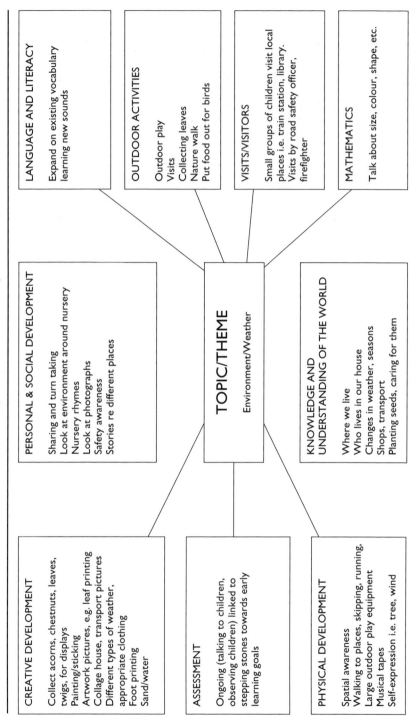

LANGUAGE AND LITERACY

Expand on existing vocabulary
learning new sounds

OUTDOOR ACTIVITIES

Outdoor play
Visits
Collecting leaves
Nature walk
Put food out for birds

VISITS/VISITORS

Small groups of children visit local
places i.e. train station, library.
Visits by road safety officer,
firefighter

MATHEMATICS

Talk about size, colour, shape, etc.

PERSONAL & SOCIAL DEVELOPMENT

Sharing and turn taking
Look at environment around nursery
Nursery rhymes
Look at photographs
Safety awareness
Stories re different places

TOPIC/THEME

Environment/Weather

KNOWLEDGE AND
UNDERSTANDING OF THE WORLD

Where we live
Who lives in our house
Changes in weather, seasons
Shops, transport
Planting seeds, caring for them

CREATIVE DEVELOPMENT

Collect acorns, chestnuts, leaves,
twigs, for displays
Painting/sticking
Artwork pictures, e.g. leaf printing
Collage house, transport pictures
Different types of weather,
appropriate clothing
Foot printing
Sand/water

ASSESSMENT

Ongoing (talking to children,
observing children) linked to
stepping stones towards early
learning goals

PHYSICAL DEVELOPMENT

Spatial awareness
Walking to places, skipping, running,
Large outdoor play equipment
Musical tapes
Self-expression i.e. tree, wind

Table 3.2 Reception class medium-term plan for history strand of eight-week topic 'Our environment' (weeks 1–3 shown)

Subject: History		Year group Reception			Topic link (if any) Around and About Our School	
Week	Learning objectives: children should learn	Knowledge, skills and understanding	Learning outcomes children should be able to:	Suggested activities	Resources	Assessment
1	To understand and use the language associated with the passing of time: Morning, Dinnertime, Afternoon. To sequence events in their own lives.	KSU 1A/1B ELG To find out about past & present events in own lives.	To sequence photographs in order showing their daily school routines in chronological order. To talk about events in their school day using the language frames. 'In the morning we … At dinner time I ….'.	Take photographs showing key times/events in the school day sequence with the class modelling the language. In the morning we … etc. Circle time – at dinnertime I … This morning I … Introduce use of past tense language. Independent activities	Camera Photographs Teddy for circle time Dictaphone to record good language models Teacher developed worksheet.	Look at ability to sequence and to place events in time order. Teaching assistant to assess use of past tense vocabulary/time related vocabulary.
2	To identify and describe own past experiences or communicate through drawing/writing. To use recall skills to recognise key dates in special remembered events in own life. To use other sources of information to find out about their past.	KSU 4B ELG To find out about past & present events in own lives.	To talk about their own past experiences. To use recall skills to remember events and feelings from a special day.	Key text: Edward's First Day at School. Read story and discuss children's own feelings about their 1st day at school. How did they feel at the beginning/end of the day. What did they do on their first day? Did this change how they felt?	Photographs taken of children on their first day. Work from children's first day. Text: Edward's First Day at School by Rosemary Wells.	Link with PSE. Are children able to identify and describe own emotions?
3	To listen to the past experiences of their peers and a family adult in school. To communicate their understanding of a special event in their own past. To look at evidence from their own past to find out information.	KSU 4B/5 ELG To find out about past and present events in own lives.	To listen to the past experiences of others and find out about the past of a known adult. To use recall skills to communicate their own past experiences. Suggested activities	Read the section: 'The First Day'. Tell the children you are going to make a book all about their first day, you want them to remember what they did. Tell them about your first day at school. Look at photographs/pieces of work from their first day. Ask them to describe what they did.	Text: Starting School, Janet & Allan Ahlberg Big book (to hold display work) Photographs Pieces of work from children in class.	Can they answer questions about their own past? Use recall skills to describe what their past experiences are. Product assessment. Can they draw to communicate understanding?

Table 3.3 Year 1 medium-term plan for history strand of eight week topic, 'Our environment' (weeks 1–3 shown)

Subject History   **Year group** One   **Topic link (if any)** Around and About Our School and Grounds

Week	Learning objectives: children should learn	Knowledge, skills and understanding	Learning outcomes: children be able:	Suggested activities	Resources	Assessment
1	To recognize the language associated with the measurement of time in relation to the concept of a 'year'. To place events in chronological order.	KSU: 1A, 1B 6d Events	To recognize and use the terms associated with a 'year'; including 'months of the year'; including a revision of the terms 'before' 'after'. To place a special event in their own life in sequential order in relation to timeline.	Read from choice of texts; discuss birthdays, how we know how old we are. Encourage children to discuss in pairs their memories from their last birthday. Can they recall their birthday month? Sequence months of year. Children to place card in order of corresponding month.	*Kipper's Birthday*, Inkpen, 1999 (London: Hodder & Stoughton) *Ruff* – Jane Hissey Year timeline Individual cards to place on timeline.	RKP – which children can recite/know names of months of year? Respond to questions using language 'before', 'after', 'older', 'younger'.
2	To listen to and respond to the past experiences of others. How to answer questions about the past. How to use a source to find out about the past.	KSU: 2B, 4A, 4B 6c Special people	To respond to oral history from a familiar adult. To recognize that we can find out about the past in different ways (ie using AVA). To answer questions about the past experiences of a special person in school.	Who are special people? Brainstorm who is special to them. Why will they/do they remember them? Focus on 'parents'. Teachers to tell story from parent of memories of going to school. How they got there, what they did etc. Listen/respond to memories of special person 'Miss Williams' memories of school.	Recording from parent. Video of Miss Williams. Questionnaire for parents.	RKP – Note children who can answer questions from information gained through listening to oral history. Product Assessment through writing/drawing.
3	How to devise and ask questions about the past. How to use different sources of information to find out about the past. To communicate through drawing what they have found out.	KSU: 4A, 4B, 5 6d Events 6c Special people	To ask questions about the past experience of others. To use different sources of information to answer questions about the past.	Parents questionnaire review. Oral history from parent. Focus on using information to answer questions. How did they get to school? What games did they play? What food did they eat? Encourage children to devise own questions to ask parent.	Visit from parent. Completed questionnaires. Questions cards as prompts. Tape recorder. Dictaphone.	RKP – Can they formulate own questions to ask about the past?

Table 3.4 Year 2 medium-term plan for history strand of eight week topic, 'Our environment' (weeks 1–3 shown)

Programme of study	Focused learning objective	Activities/organization/Adult involvement	Resources
Week 1			
2a) Recognize why people did things, why events happened and what happened as a result.	To gain an understanding of the passage of time through story.	Links with literacy hour for this week Asha in the Attic. Introduce the children to the book From Me to You. Read the blurb carefully to the children and explain the different events over the passing time.	From Me to You, Rodgers (1997)
2b) Identify differences between ways of life at different times.		Explain that this is one person's story and that we can find out about the past from different sources e.g. non-fiction texts, newspapers, video footage, photographs, etc.	Worksheet
6a) Changes in their own lives and the way of life of their family or others around them.	To place events from the story in chronological order.	Read the story to the children and discuss the illustrations – what's going on, clothes, furnishings, etc. Record 3 key events in the grandmother's story.	
Week 2			
2a) Recognize why people did things, why events happened and what happened as a result.	To ask questions in order to gain an understanding of the past.	Read the story from last week again and recall main events. Teacher to show children photographs of won grandparents and talk about memories of them from when a child.	Class teacher's photographs of own grandparents.
2b) Identify differences between ways of life at different times.		Tell children that they are going to find out something about the other children's grandparents and discuss types of questions to ask etc.	From Me to You
6a) Changes in their own lives and the way of life of their family or others around them.		Ask children to talk in pairs about their own grandmothers and then report back to whole class something that they found out about the other person's grandma.	
Week 3			
4a) How to find out about the past from a range of sources of information.	To understand the passing of time and to become familiar with first hand accounts of events.	Visit to school from travelling company Tempus Fugit. Explain to children the meaning of tempus fugit. Presentation of a grandfather's story.	Company – Tempus Fugit
4b) To ask and answer questions about the past.		The follow-up work from this experience will be done through the Literacy Hour during the rest of the week. (See Literacy planning).	
2a) Recognise why people did things, why events happened and what happened as a result.			

Table 3.5 Progression in the development of historical knowledge, skills and concepts from the Foundation Stage to Key Stage 1

Nursery	Reception	Year 1	Year 2
Expand on existing vocabulary/ learning new sounds; Nursery rhymes	Listening station with rhymes in English and Gujerati *(ELG Language for Communication)	Listening and responding to rhymes (NLS)	
Can name the time of day associated with various activities	To talk about events in their school day, using language forms ... in the morning we ...; To understand and use the term 'yesterday'	To recognize and use terms, years, months of the year, before/after	
To look at the environment around nursery; Where we live ... who lives in our house; Changes in time, plant growth, weather seasons		To identify and consider the concept of change from visual/physical evidence – outdoor history trail	
Looking at photographs	Looking at photographs showing key events in the school day; Photographs of the school day; Photographs of their first day at school for evidence	To use photographic evidence of change using SMART board and to discuss of changes that are occurring today	Using a photo of a teacher's grandmother for evidence
Recognizing differences through hand prints	Looking in mirror, recording details (evidence of) change – height, handprints, footprints	To place special events in their own life in sequential order on a time line	To begin to see personal history and family history within a wider context; Class timeline and individual timelines to show date of birth child/grandparent, date they will go to junior school; Record 3 key events in grandmother's story
To follow a sequence	To review events pictorially from a story, 'A Very Hot Day'; To use recall skills to remember events and feelings from a special day; To place events in chronological order; To develop sequencing skills; Re-tell narratives in correct order	To recall their birthday month and sequence months of the year; Reviewing sequencing, retelling story and sequencing illustrations	

Table 3.5 (continued)

Nursery	Reception	Year 1	Year 2
Tell what happens next in a simple story Listen attentively to and enjoy a story	After the story *Edwards First Day at School* to discuss their own first day Teacher to talk about her first day	To describe changes in the character in the story *Threadbear*	To gain an understanding of the passing of time through stories: *From Me to You* and *Asha in the Attic* (NLS). To explain that this is one person's story and that we can find out about the past from different sources To become familiar with first hand accounts: Tempus Fugit Theatre Group – *Beth's Story* – grandparent/evacuation and *The Patchwork Quilt* – evidence of memories
To become more inquisitive Encourage children to ask questions and describe reasons	To find out about past experience of one known adult	Via class museum of their own old artefacts to recognize the concept of oldness and to develop skills using their own special objects To ask questions about the past experience of others (via parental questionnaires)	Child to bring in objects from their past and talk about their own memories. To discuss types of questions to ask grandparents (via questionnaire)

Table 3.6 Perceived problems in developing continuity from the Foundation Stage to Key Stage 1 and some possible solutions

Problems	Possible solutions
History as a boxed subject on the timetable	Teacher creativity, flexibility within a structured framework
Lack of time Constraints of National Literacy Strategy, National Numeracy Strategy	Using history based text in literacy hour with later direct history teaching Some integrated thematic work whilst maintaining the integrity of the subject through careful planning
Lack of freedom to respond to the spontaneous due to timetable	An element of teacher freedom relating to when 'subjects' can be taught Whole school policy which allocates one hour (or more if possible) for movement of timetabled subjects e.g. so NLS can take place later morning/afternoon if allocated time is needed
Ensuring progression from Foundation to Key Stage 1	Liaison between feeder playgroups, nurseries, reception and Key Stage 1 teachers Access to documents related to planning and evaluations
Children who have no, little or restricted access to grandparents	Use of story related to grandparents' time, drama group presentation, prepared audio/video taped, e-mailed photographs, visiting speaker

Introduction: spying out the land

We had planned that our third study, to take place during the autumn term of 2001, would have a humanities focus and that in addition to the usual mathematics and language strand it would include a physical education dimension. This would mean that aspects of all the areas of learning and subjects would then have been included in our book. During the summer Chris Sixsmith contacted a dynamic and enthusiastic head teacher, Anne Dubois, at Market Gates Infants' School. Anne is always interested in new initiatives. Her school is a three-class entry infants' school in the centre of a large northern city, and the children come from a diverse range of ethnic backgrounds. 'Our school theme for the autumn term will be the environment', Anne said, 'and yes, we'd love to work with you.'

Although Market Gates Infants has its own nursery class, Anne was keen to also include in the project the pre-school playgroup in St Mark's day care centre a little further down the road, which is run by the social services. She introduced Chris Sixsmith to her colleague Jean Rutter, director of the centre. Jean said that the playgroup would also be happy to work on the environment theme in the autumn term.

So on a mild grey afternoon in October, after the school and the college had established the patterns of the new term, six college Early Years tutors, Neil Simco (geography), Jim Lavin (physical education), Margaret Foster (mathematics), Christine Cooper (history – with a special interest in the links between history and language) and the editors, Hilary Cooper and Chris Sixsmith, were all pressing the buzzer at Market Gates Infants' School. Market Gates is a gabled, single-storey, red-brick building at the junction of two roads, one an arterial road busy with shops and traffic and the other a street of terraced houses. The school is separated from the roads by typical nineteenth-century iron railings.

'Welcome to Market Gates School' proclaimed the signs in Gujerati, Urdu and several other languages – and welcome we immediately felt. Anne was doing a million things as usual but found time greet us. 'Yes, isn't the embroidered elephant lovely – and do you like these snail paintings? They were done by two boys in reception – they mixed all the colours themselves – it took them about three weeks – on and off!' Patsy Roebuck, the PE coordinator, rushed through the hall in her tracksuit. Helen Bawtry introduced herself as the geography and literacy coordinator and Andrea Holmes as the history coordinator. Helen collected us all around a large horseshoe table on luxurious blue upholstered swivel chairs, and organized tea and biscuits. Old acquaintanceships were renewed and new ones begun amidst a lot of chatter. Then Anne arrived with Jean Rutter and her playgroup colleague, Monica Maden.

Hilary Cooper and Chris Sixsmith outlined the aims and organization of the project. Jean said that activities in the playgroup would fit in well with the environment theme, but she was anxious to point out the many ways in which her playgroup setting is different from a nursery class in a school. We were all accustomed to working in schools, but everyone, including Anne, was fascinated – and humbled – as Jean talked about her playgroup in the day care unit.

ST MARK'S DAY CARE UNIT PRE-SCHOOL PLAYGROUP

Jean explained:

> Our work in the St Mark's social services day care unit is concerned mainly with supporting families. The day care has been reduced by 5 per cent – that's roughly two or three children each day. Ours is an area of great social deprivation. The priority for most of our families is just getting through the day. There are all sorts of social difficulties. Often a crisis overrides the educational activities we had planned. Today, for example, a child was taken into care. Often parents just don't have the energy to support their children's learning, yet education is the children's only way out. So we run groups for parents and try to encourage them to get involved in their children's play. And we take education out into the community: for example, we run play sessions at a hostel for the homeless where otherwise the children would have no opportunities for play. Our team at the unit consists of myself, my deputy, Sally Soames, who is our senior nursery officer, and eight nursery officers: four concerned with social care and four, Monica Maden, Joan Greaves, Garry Groves and Bindi Patel, with education.

MARKET GATES INFANTS' SCHOOL

'I often phone Jean. We get lots of insights into our children and their circumstances through the playgroup', Anne told us. She explained that

Market Gates is organized to provide the structure and the focuses which children may otherwise lack. Learning and assessment are rooted in play experiences that are developed through the key areas of the curriculum, so that children gradually learn how to think in the different ways which characterize each subject.

Each class has a role-play room, and there are also three 'subject rooms': one for literary activities, one for mathematics activities and one for science and design and technology. Each subject room is set up and managed by the subject coordinator who is supported by a nursery nurse. Each class spends part of each day in its role-play room. For the remaining three sessions they move, with their teacher, to each of the subject rooms in rotation. In each subject room the children undertake and develop activities stimulated by their role-play area. Anne showed us large handmade books displaying selections of their resulting cross-curricular work. One class had created a hotel in their role-play area. Another was currently working with the builders (real ones) to decorate a 'new room' that was being built. They had stripped the walls in one area, designed new wallpaper, measured the walls to find out how much paper was needed, printed the repeating patterns on the paper, made it into rolls of equal length, costed it, written invoices and bills, and were finally putting it on the walls. 'The builders have been given strict instructions that this wall must not be touched', Anne said. 'It is a permanent part of our new room.'

After this vivid digression to illustrate how the school organization works in practice, Anne explained the built-in progression in the ways that children's learning is monitored, assessed and extended. When children are in the reception class and Year 1 practical opportunities for assessing literacy and numeracy skills are set up by the nursery nurse in the role-play area. In Year 2, the teacher identifies concepts for development in the subject rooms, based on their perceived needs.

The chill-out area

'As you can see from my tracksuit, my specialism is history', Jim announced. (He had so far been uncharacteristically quiet.) Anne was reassuring. 'You needn't feel left out, Jim. We are the only school in Lancashire to be selected to take part in a new QCA initiative to develop a zone park area. It will have a garden cage, a court for ball games and an activities area. There will be all sorts of activities set out, connected by a heart line – a line painted on the ground, in the shape of a heart, which leads the children through the various zones and activities to remind them that keeping active will help them keep fit. We've got poor attendance, you see, and the QCA thought that this might encourage children to come to school. And we've got Nike sponsorship. I expect the lunch-time supervisors will have Nike baseball caps!' (Mock palpitations of excitement from Jim!) It was a complete coincidence that the QCA project fitted in so well with ours. 'You'll be seeing a lot of me', Jim warned.

WHAT DO ST MARK'S DAY CARE UNIT PRE-SCHOOL PLAYGROUP AND MARKET GATES INFANTS' SCHOOL WANT FROM THE PROJECT?

Jean Rutter had to leave the meeting promptly, in order to accompany a distressed parent to the doctor's surgery, but before leaving she identified two benefits she hoped for from the project. First, she hoped it would help her staff to refocus on the educational dimension of their work. 'We really are crisis-led. Yet we need to re-establish the importance of providing educational activities for our children.' Second, she hoped we would try to engage with and involve the parents, maybe by talking to them informally about their children's activities, to try to help them enjoy and value their work at school: 'Perhaps we could ask them about their problems and their children's.' Jean left informing us that 'The parents' coffee morning is on Thursdays!'

Anne felt that – in addition to the bonus of Jim's involvement in the new chill-out area, and Neil Simco and Christine Cooper's contribution to the humanities dimension of the environment topic – she and her staff would gain so much from greater insights into the work of the playgroup. 'Usually we really only have time to liase over problems', she said. 'I think we'd better all read the book!'

The meeting concluded with an agreement that the school and playgroup would send the college tutors their medium-term plans by the end of the half-term break and exchange contact addresses so that the tutors could make arrangements to return to work with the children during the three weeks following the holiday. The playgroup outline plan for the environment theme is shown in Table 3.1. Tables 3.2, 3.3 and 3.4 show the first three weeks of the history strand of Market Gates' medium-term plans.

As we left Anne was still pointing out the stages in the planning and design of the fruit and flower collages along the hall wall. 'Look at the lines of that seed case – we only use black and white in the literacy room because we feel that stimulates a richer vocabulary.' 'We had a wonderful music day last week', added Sally Tomkinson, her deputy, newly emerged from tutorials with our students currently on placement at Market Gates. 'We had an African drummer – all day! Did you see the way Raymond captured the curl of the brakete drumstick in his painting? You can still "do" music and art. That's what feeds the skills across the curriculum.'

It had been a stimulating meeting, everyone agreed, as we made our way back past the iron railings and the pushchairs and the women in their brightly coloured saris.

Chapter 11

History: finding out about the past and the language of time

Christine Cooper

This chapter considers ways in which playgroup staff and teachers can use the early learning goals and meet the requirements of the Key Stage 1 history curriculum. It provides an example of the way in which one school meets national requirements while maintaining a place for teachers' creativity to respond to the needs of the children.

In these days of an objectives-led curriculum it is easy to overlook the ways in which children acquire information about words and their meanings, and the ways in which languages are organized. Children have a substantial bank of knowledge about language by the time they begin nursery or playgroup. They acquire this through their daily interactions as they listen and talk to family, friends and other carers, as they absorb information through storybooks and from their observations of daily life. Information, skills and concepts relating to 'history' evolve from children's daily experience. In St Mark's day care unit the groups changed from day to day, with some children attending only one or two days a week. The staff were concerned to extend the pupils' knowledge of language and especially their 'knowledge and understanding of the world' in a way that reflected the 'natural' ways in which children acquire knowledge and understandings.

ST MARK'S DAY CARE UNIT PRE-SCHOOL PLAYGROUP

The *Curriculum Guidance for the Foundation Stage* lists, albeit in a formal way, the many experiences that Early Years practitioners consider an essential part of a child's early experience. Planting seeds and discussing growth, observing and discussing changes in the seasons, learning nursery rhymes and listening to stories – all these provide informal ways of developing and extending language. They also provide a platform from which historical understandings (passing of time sequences, then/now and evidence of change) can develop.

A range of photographs was used in the playgroup to get children to talk, discuss and make inferences; yet, by their very nature, photographs represent the past. This informal meeting with visual sources provides a basis from which to progress to the National Curriculum Knowledge, Skills and Understanding 4: using photographs as historical evidence.

For children, listening to and joining in nursery rhymes and stories provide a valuable and enjoyable experience as well as an opportunity to feel part of a group. It also provides a basis from which children's understanding of semantics and syntax can develop. In *History in the Early Years* (2002), Hilary Cooper suggests that '[l]anguage is the tool for unlocking the past'. Nursery rhymes are included in the early learning goals for communication, language and literacy (DFEE/QCA 2000); they also contribute to children's historical understanding as they introduce them to language through scenes from the past. Jayne Woodhouse (2001: 18) draws attention to the ways in which traditional rhymes provide opportunities for children to discover old occupations (e.g. candlestick maker, miller). Many illustrations for rhymes show types of dress, housing and farming which reflect the past.

It is through their planning, the creation of learning objectives, the language they use and the questions they ask that playgroup staff and Key Stage 1 teachers can extend these experiences to bring about the starting points from which later historical understanding, skills and concepts can develop.

On the day of my visit to St Mark's playgroup, children were listening and responding to the popular story *We're Going on a Bear Hunt* (Rosen 1996). The characters in the story retrace their steps, and this provided Joan Greaves, the play leader, with the opportunity to draw attention to the sequence of the story, and the reverse of the sequence as the characters run away from the bear. Joan Greaves's evaluation of her work identified themes, later used by the Infant's School, covering the child, the family and the local environment:

> We talked about our feet and how they were all different.
> The children loved talking about where they lived and their families.
> The children enjoyed talking about the buildings in the street.
> The children have painted pictures of the local mosque.

CONTINUITY FROM PLAYGROUP TO KEY STAGE 1

Reflecting Jerome Bruner's notion of a spiral curriculum, Table 3.6 illustrates how, in order to progress in acquiring historical knowledge, skills and concepts, the children revisit those areas which are identified in the early learning goals and National Curriculum for history.

Three years ago I undertook a school-based research project to discover whether the ideals set down in the 1967 Plowden Report, of a spontaneous and integrated approach to learning which starts with the interests of the child, were dead. It was Market Gates School, among others, which provided evidence that some legacy of Plowden remained. There, displays of individual's art work, emergent writing and class books were – and still are – everywhere, as children's individuality is celebrated. As Catherine Harris, a class teacher, said:

> Their drawings and their art work are their own. You can see it's an individual child's work because they are all completely different. We respond to what they produce and the questions to each child are different.

Apparent tensions between national requirements and the philosophy of individual teachers appear resolved. The school's 'flexible, yet structured approach' (the words of Andrea Holmes, the history coordinator) provides an excellent example of how teachers who are secure in the knowledge of their subject and have collectively established a philosophy based on the perceived needs of their pupils can plan for meaningful learning experiences in history.

In the reception class there was a large frieze depicting 'My family'. A history specialist would immediately relate this to 'Knowledge and Understanding of the World (6a), changes in their own and the way of life of their families', while an English specialist might look at communication through print and an art specialist consider the use of colour and texture. Nichols and Dean (1997: 2–3) have drawn attention to the links between teachers' understanding of 'what historians do' and the teaching methods they choose. Such an understanding has important implications for planning for progression and an awareness of the ways in which a flexible yet structured approach can result. At Market Gates School both the history coordinator, Andrea Holmes, and Jill Reeve, the reception teacher with whom I worked, had history degrees. Each had followed a course that was a preparation for subject leaders in history.

Jeffrey and Woods (1996) have drawn attention to the ways in which teachers have felt deprofessionalized as they have sought to mediate government policies in the light of their own philosophies. Fortunately, for Key Stage 1 history there is little prescription. The 'breadth of study' that is the required content begins with the children's immediate experience and works backwards, reflecting the English tradition of the Plowden Report.

With the playgroup and local school choosing 'the environment' as the theme for the autumn term, a way has been found to gradually build up children's historical knowledge, concepts and skills. The staff have made personal choices and professional judgements based on their understanding of how children think and learn, their knowledge of the children and the nature of their subject. This study provides one illustration of how a school can meet the statutory requirements at Key Stage 1 while maintaining a flexible approach that reflects the long-standing tenets of English primary education.

MARKET GATES INFANTS' SCHOOL

Market Gates Infants' School interpreted the environment theme as 'Around and about our school'. Children considered themselves, their parents, other adults in the community and grandparents. They looked for evidence of change and continuity.

The reception class: sequencing the school day

Displays and class books in the reception class reflected the theme of myself, the family and the Three Bears. There were many books containing children's work, many of which had specific links with the development of historical understanding. When working on a theme of the Three Bears, the children were introduced to the idea that a suitcase provides evidence related to a person and an event.

Sequencing the school day

Since history is about time it is important that children develop the language of time and that they begin to build up an understanding of the passing of time. Jill Reeve, the reception class teacher, had used a digital camera to take photographs of her class in different locations, engaged in different activities at specific times in the school day. The children recognized them immediately. Coloured photographs were introduced individually. The task was made easier as children in this school change rooms for specific activities. Here, the children were using photographs as evidence of past yet recent times. This was a development from the more informal use of photographs in the playgroup. As she introduced each photograph the teacher asked questions and made comments that encouraged and prompted deductions based on the evidence.

Mrs Reeve:	What do you think is going on here?
Ben:	We're going home.
Mrs Reeve:	When do you bring in coats?
Kylie:	In the morning.
Mrs Reeve:	So this photo shows you in the morning. What's happening here?
Monsoor:	We're walking and running.
John:	We have bicycles.

Mrs Reeve: So?
Monsoor, John: It's playtime!

The class appeared very eager to answer questions and excited by seeing themselves in the photographs. The digital camera was an excellent resource for making photographs of the recent past. The complication of photographs showing similar events – for example different playtimes – provided the opportunity for an element of deduction based on the children noticing small details, such as different people looking after them at morning play and at lunch time. Individuals volunteered to go to the whiteboard to place specific photographs in sequence. Throughout the session the children were engaged in talking, questioning, answering questions and making choices. Links with literacy were particularly apparent in the case of a group creating zigzag books to illustrate activities associated with different times. They were working with a bilingual assistant, Savitri Tapur, who used both Gujerati and English to encourage children to talk, make deductions, write and consider phoneme/grapheme relationships. Both Savitri Tapur and Jill Reeve structured their questions in a similar manner to target words and phrases such as 'after', 'before', 'then we', 'what do we do next?' (National Curriculum Knowledge, Skills and Understanding [hereafter, NC, KSU] 1b).

Working with the teacher, another group used a selection of the photographs to sequence and, interestingly, the teacher extended the activities and asked the children to consider the sounds they were likely to hear. Here, the use of an audio tape recorder was able to provide an extension or alternative way of considering sequencing.

Year 1: changes around and about our school

As the term had progressed, the children in Andrea Holme's Year 1 class had consolidated and extended their sequencing work, moving from 'our day' to months, special events and creating a timeline of their life. They had been introduced to the idea of memories and, through the innovative use of audio and video recordings, begun finding out about school life in the past as experienced by a parent or another older person. Information had been gathered from parents using a questionnaire, and one had visited the school to talk to the children. The idea of 'finding out the past from using evidence' was extended through the use of artefacts connected with the oral history. After using a non-fiction text *The School*, children followed a history trail around the school grounds, identifying old and new objects.

Gradually, through using the story *Threadbear* (Inkpen 1990) and the creation of a class museum of objects brought in by the teachers and children, the concepts of 'old' and 'change' became the focus of history lessons. One important aspect that was introduced was the idea that what was old to a child could appear relatively new to an older person.

The playground: seizing the moment

The lesson I watched built on these experiences by returning to oral history in the context of changes in the school playground. At the time it was undergoing change due to work being carried out by QCA supported by Nike. Possible results had been discussed with the children. However, the class teacher, Andrea Holmes, could not have predicted that during a timetabled lesson on 29 September 2001 such exciting things would have been happening in the playground: diggers were in action, workers were dashing around with spades, and a roller was flattening tarmac.

There is a long tradition in English education of making use of the spontaneous event:

> When a class of seven-year-olds notice the birds that come to the bird table, outside the classroom window, they may decide, after discussion with their teacher, to make their own aviary.
>
> (Plowden 1967: 542)

National requirements have created tensions for teachers when rich, exciting, motivating events occur, and yet they feel constrained by recent changes brought about by the SATS (Standard Assessment Tasks), the National Literacy Strategy and the National Numeracy Strategy:

> We never have time to listen to children when they come in with 'I did this' or 'Here's a book' or 'I found this twig'.
>
> (Galton et al. 1999: 179)

Andrea Holmes, the history coordinator, explained how the school managed to resolve such tensions and allow the children to benefit from the first-hand experience that results from teachers being aware of the possibilities of using the spontaneous:

> There is a lot of flexibility in the school but it is part of a structured vision. We have term-based topics, not a yearly cycle, but they are not set in stone. We get together as a school and make and discuss our aims and then decide the basis for our decisions.

Using memories of the bilingual teacher Susmita Weaver, photographic evidence and the children's observations of how changes were occurring at the very time the lesson was taking place, Andrea Holmes made use of the class's interest to engage with the main historical concepts of evidence, change and continuity, cause and effect. Building on their previous learning, the key term 'memory' formed the focus of much of the lesson. In introducing the session, Susmita Weaver reminded the class of the kinds of evidence that could be used to find out about the past and the way in which things change.

Mrs. Weaver outlined the differences in the playground of ten years ago:

- No murals, only brick walls;
- No gate;
- No separate areas for different year groups to play in;
- No fences;
- No tubs with plants;
- No benches, children had to sit on the ground;
- No garden;
- No containers for play equipment;
- No bridge;
- No climbing frame.

The children were particularly interested in what they could find in the playground that had been there in 1991. Imran identified some faded yellow lines on the playground which had been stronger ten years ago. The children were keen to ask questions.

Wassim:	Did you have one bench?
Mrs Weaver:	I think it's still in the same place
Alisa:	Didn't they have any toys?
Lee:	If the children had no toys, what did they play with?
Mrs Weaver:	Footballs from home, catch, skipping ropes and they made up their own games.

Andrea Holmes then introduced a memory bubble for the year 1991. The children moved to look and discuss photographs showing 2001 – before the changes began. Here the use of an interactive whiteboard was invaluable. As in the reception class, the use of digital pictures allowed very recent pictures to be used. Differentiated group work resulted in a whole-class session around a three-piece whiteboard;

1991	2001	2011
Memory bubble	Photograph + children's drawings resulting from their trip to the playground with a teaching assistant	Children's drawings and writings to inform head teacher of what they would like to see in 2011

During this lesson, the children had considered a range of evidence related to 'then and now'. They were developing a repertoire of ways in which they could investigate the past (NC, KSU 4: the strand of Knowledge, Skills and Understanding in the history National Curriculum concerned with historical enquiry). They had also been introduced to the idea of why changes

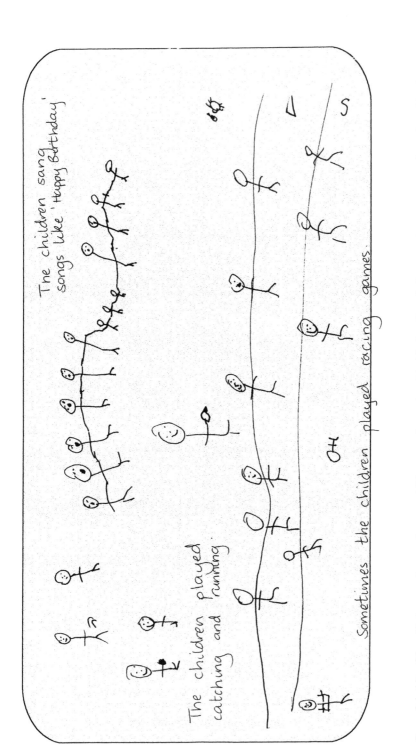

Figure 3.1 Alisa (Year 1) drew a picture of games children may have played in Market Gates' playground ten years ago (Learning objective: to respond to oral history; to show an understanding of events in the past through illustrations)

What is happening in the playground today?

Figure 3.2 Sarah (Year 1) drew what was happening in the playground today (Learning objective: to discuss, identify and record changes in the immediate locality)

History Year One Aamirah.

What changes would you like to make?

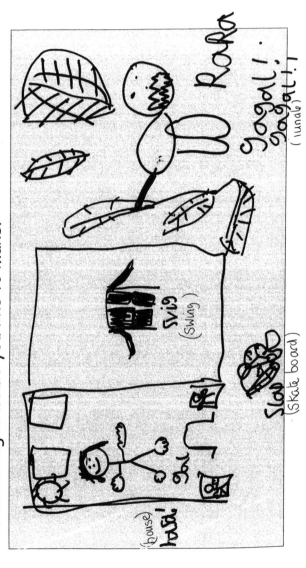

Figure 3.3 Aanrah (Year 1) suggested ideas for the new playground (Learning objective: to identify and discuss change in relation to the school environment; to use appropriate tense and vocabulary during discussion)

occur (NC, KSU 2a: the strand of historical understanding in the National Curriculum concerned with change, with understanding why events happened and what happened as a result). Since they were going to take their suggestions to the head teacher they became aware of how they as individuals had the potential to influence change. Figures 3.1, 3.2, and 3.3 show how these Year 1 children illustrated their developing understanding of time and change. Progression from reception had been achieved through a consolidation of sequencing work and an extension of the variety of evidence which had been used. Although a large amount of Year 1 work was concerned with the children's experience, they had progressed and become aware that you can find out about the past from older people, artefacts and the built environment.

Year 2: grandparents' time, the extended use of evidence

The planning for history at Year 2 extended work on 'the lives of the children and familiar adults'. Reception experience related to 'Myself'; Year 1 had made use of evidence from the children's parents' generation; Year 2 children progressed to looking at ways in which they could find out about their grandparents' time. Although not explicitly linked to the built environment, the theme provided opportunities for children to explore memories from those in the community around and about the school.

The plans (Table 3.4) show the ways in which children's knowledge of 'how we can find out about the past' will be extended by revisiting primary sources such as photographs and meeting new sources such as newspapers. A knowledge of the different ways in which the past is represented (National Curriculum, Key Element 3) is to be developed through the use of fiction and a visiting drama group. The play provided strong links with the National Literacy Strategy and specific plans had been created showing the links between the subjects.

Apart from the natural links between English and history (Hoodless 1998), the use of historical stories to implement aspects of the National Literacy Strategy allows good use of time when little is available for non-core subjects. In Year 2, emphasis had been placed on the use of story, with texts including *Asha in the Attic* (Powling 2000), *From Me to You* (Rogers 1995), *The Patchwork Quilt* (Flournoy 1995) and *Beth's Story*, a drama production dealing with the evacuation of children during World War Two. This had been used as a starting point to enable the children to find out about the time of their grandparents and older people. Jo Barkham (2002) has explained in detail how *Asha in the Attic* can be used with Year 2 pupils to develop both literacy skills and historical enquiry using sources.

The skills of sequencing and using evidence such as photographs, oral history and artefacts were revisited. Interviews were added to questionnaires as the pupils increased their skills of enquiry to find out about their grandparents' times. They were introduced to the idea that there would be a range of evidence resulting from the differing experiences of individuals.

The emphasis on 'grandparents' in Key Stage 1 history can cause problems for those who have no grandparents and for those children, such as many in this school, whose grandparents do not live in this country. Here the drama group's telling of *Grandfather's Story* was helpful as all had access to the story. It also provided an opportunity to introduce National Curriculum KSU3 and the complex concept of drama as interpretation.

The play about evacuation provided a good opportunity for children to meet new ideas and unfamiliar words. Misconceptions in history lessons are often associated with language as children try to make sense of a new word in the light of their existing knowledge. In this case the teacher, Helen Bawtry, found that the word 'evacuation' had been interpreted by one child as 'evicted' and by another as 'vacuumed'.

With the coming of a subject-based National Curriculum, many schools have allocated specific times for history. The Year 2 teacher had chosen to split her session on *The Patchwork Quilt* into two so that she could introduce the story and invite the children to bring in evidence of their own special memories on the following day.

Using the story: The Patchwork Quilt

The Patchwork Quilt is the story of a West Indian grandmother discussing her memories prompted by the squares of material she is using to make a quilt. The children's interest was aroused immediately, as Helen Bawtry used every opportunity to introduce the lesson by using sources from her past. A large group photograph showing her own grandmother, her memories of visiting the seaside as a child, references to artefacts they had already seen such as her great-grandmother's jewellery – all these combined to win the children's interest. Related questions and comments allowed a revision of the term 'memory' and the children were very adept at discussing the concept of 'the past'.

Mrs Bawtry: History is about the past.
Zeb: Yesterday.
Yasmeen: Like this morning.
Zaheer: It's not cold now, the cold has passed.

The impact of the lesson and the ways in which the class made sense of the experiences teachers had planned were demonstrated afterwards when children spontaneously referred to things they had done that day as 'now in the past'. As one child passed the science room he said: 'We've done science. That's now in the past.'

In preparation for the story, Helen Bawtry brought in a quilt she was making and referred to the materials linked with memories.

Mrs Bawtry: This is from a skirt I used to wear.
Kirsty: But it doesn't fit you now [suggesting a reason why it was no longer worn].
Mrs Bawtry: This is from my grandma's apron. She was always baking. The fabric helps me remember.
Aisha: You imagine that.

With great excitement the next day the children returned with articles from their past, ranging from Saline's baby blanket and Gunny's first earring to Jason's Babygro, which the tall owner referred to as his 'nightie'. This caused great excitement as Jason held this against himself to illustrate how he had altered in size.

CONCLUSION

The liaison between the playgroup and the school illustrates one way in which starting points for history begun in the informal atmosphere of the playgroup can be developed. Increased history-related vocabulary, practice at making deductions and querying evidence led to an increasing understanding of the major historical concepts of change, continuity, causation, enquiry and interpretation. In all the classes the children were highly motivated, interested and keen to contribute verbally, through their writing and by bringing their own ideas, experiences and artefacts related to the topic. This resulted from teachers using their professional knowledge and selecting the teaching and learning methods they considered best for their children.

SOME SUGGESTIONS FOR FURTHER WORK

With reception children

Use a digital camera to make recent photographs related to the children's experience and encourage them to look closely for evidence that allows them to sequence the events.

Consider using songs which tell a story to assist the children in sequence work, for example: 'A Fox Jumped Up', 'I Know an Old Lady Who Swallowed a Fly'.

Use the illustrations from traditional nursery rhymes or storybooks to introduce children to the concept of change: for example, in dress, houses, occupations or other ways in which the past is represented.

With Year 1 and Year 2

Experiment with the use of audiotapes and video recordings for oral history.

Consider creating a video that will support local history trails or site work, for example around your school or local area. This could be used for preparation and follow-up work or if you have to cancel a field trip because of bad weather.

Experiment with using a SMART board (see p. 172) to provide images of artefacts, or photographs of the locality showing now/then from which the children can make deductions

USEFUL BOOKS

Hoodless, P. (ed.) (1998) *History and English in the Primary School: Exploiting the Links*, London: Routledge.

Provides many examples of the ways in which history and English are linked. Through research examples and case studies it provides a really practical basis from which to develop history teaching while being aware of the ways in which the special relationship that exists between the two subjects can be used to advantage. Covers site visits, writing, storytelling, working with pictures, written sources, children's awareness of times and developing reading skills through history.

O'Hara, Mark and Lucy (2001) *Teaching History 3–11: The Essential Guide (2001)*, London: Continuum.

Aimed at those on teacher training courses and in the first year of teaching, it provides a comprehensive mixture of the theory relating to history as a subject and practical guidance. It will be invaluable to those new to the profession, who will appreciate the guidance given under headings taken from 4/98. The wider issues related to the teaching of history, such as organizing environments conducive to history teaching, children with special needs and curriculum coordination, are included.

BIBLIOGRAPHY

Cooper, H. (2002) *History in the Early Years* (2nd edn), London: Routledge.

Flournoy, V. (1995) *The Patchwork Quilt*, Harmondsworth: Puffin.

Galton, M., Hargreaves, L., Comber, C., Wall, D. and Pell, A. (1999) *Inside the Primary Classroom Twenty Years On*, London: Routledge.

Hoodless, P. (ed.) (1998) *History and English in the Primary School: Exploiting the Links*, London: Routledge.

Inkpen, M. (1990) *Threadbear*, London: Hodder & Stoughton.

Jeffrey, B. and Woods, P. (1996) 'Feeling Deprofessionalised: the Social Construction of Emotions during an OFSTED inspection', *Cambridge Journal of Education*, 26: 3.

Nicols, J. and Dean, J. (1997) *History 7–11*, London: Routledge.

Powling, C. (2000) *Asha in the Attic*, Oxford: Rigby Red Giant.

Barkham, J. in Powling, C. (2002) 'A Book for the Literacy Hour' in *Primary History* 31, 24–25.
Rogers, P. (1995) *From Me to You*, London: Orchard.
Rosen, M. (1996) *We're Going on a Bear Hunt* (big book), London: WalkerBooks.
Woodhouse, J. (2001) *Primary History 21*.

Chapter 12

Developing a geographical perspective within an integrated theme

Neil Simco

This chapter considers progression in elements of children's learning in geography from nursery to Year 2. It aims to identify aspects of children's spatial development over this period of time and to celebrate their achievements. Practical examples will demonstrate how teachers planned for and taught sequences of activities that reflect three key principles of Early Years geography education.

Although these three principles are not exclusive or even complete, they do represent major elements of what we know about young children's understanding of geographical concepts. It also follows that these principles can be translated across the early learning goals and Key Stage 1. However the curriculum is shaped at national level, it is arguable that broad learning processes in geographical education will remain. The three principles are as follows:

- It is important not to underestimate the degree of spatial knowledge which young children bring to their understanding of the world around them.
- Effective geographical education involves the integration of theme, skills and place.
- As a child's experience of learning geography develops, it is important to revisit and build on the skills and understandings acquired at earlier stages.

The chapter consists of three parts: an elaboration of the key principles; a description of children's experience of early geographical education as they work on their shared theme, the environment; and how the teachers interpret the principles.

THREE PRINCIPLES OF EARLY YEARS GEOGRAPHICAL EDUCATION

A first principle underpinning early geographical education is that it is important not to underestimate the geographical skills and abilities which young
children develop. This principle is critical: we must not use a deficit model
to represent their development in this subject. It is easy to underestimate
their ability. Much of our current understanding of children's development
in geography has its origins in Piaget's thinking and research. The difficulty
here is, as Scoffham (1998: 19) identifies, that the underestimation of the
skills and competencies of young children has 'in part been due to an uncrit-
ical acceptance of Piaget's theories'. While children pass through various
developmental stages, they do so in ways that are far more individual and
variable than Piaget's theory of learning stages suggests. The fact that children have significant spatial ability at a relatively early age has implications
for the curriculum and approaches to teaching and learning.

The main contribution of Piaget's work in relation to spatial development
focused on the concept of 'realism': the way young children comprehend the
world outside themselves (Piaget 1954), and ways in which they perceive
the positioning of objects in relation to each other (Piaget and Inhelder
1956). Piaget described three processes which together describe the child's
understanding of reality between the ages of three and eleven. The first
process is where a child develops the ability to see the interrelationships
between objects and phenomena; for example, a very young child may
believe that clouds move by themselves (Palmer 1994). Later an idea will
develop that, while they move with the wind, they still have their own direction, and still later will come the realization that there are natural forces
which determine cloud movement.

A second process is the development of the ability to see other points of
view and the gradual acquisition of the idea that reality is that which is
common to all points of view. The development of this ability is of course
essential if map skills and spatial understanding are to be acquired.

Finally, there is the gradual development of the child's ability to distin-
guish self from the physical environment. One aspect of this is participation,
the idea that events in the environment are caused by our own actions.
Palmer (1994) provides the example of a young child who believes that the
sun follows him as he walks along.

All of this translates into three stages in the development of geographical
skills (Piaget et al. 1960). At the topological stage, up to the age of about
seven, children are egocentric, and one element of their egocentrism is that
they are thought incapable of perceiving the plan view of, say, a classroom
because it is an abstract representation and not within their line of vision.
Moreover relationships between places can only be seen in relative terms,
using words such as 'near' or 'distant'. Between the ages of about seven and

ten children enter into the projective stage where they are able to see another viewpoint with the result that they can then draw a route in their own minds. Once the 'Euclidean stage' is reached, at around ten years of age, the child is able to perceive with some accuracy the relationship between objects and places enabling the drawing of a reasonably accurate map in terms of scale and distance.

The essence of Piaget's contribution to the education of young children is that they develop in uniform ways as they move through various stages of development; the impact of context is seen as relatively minor and individual difference underplayed. However, many would argue that in reality children vary enormously and that there are some younger than seven who are perfectly capable of representing certain elements of a plan view or of drawing a route map or picture map with reasonable accuracy in terms of the position of various objects or places (Halocha 1998; Scoffham 1998; Wiegand 1992). Wiegand suggests that the difficulty lies in the fact that 'the indirect effect of Piaget's work has been the widespread belief that young children are not yet "ready" for map work, whereas a growing body of evidence suggests that in the right circumstances even very young children can have success with map skills' (p. 27). The evidence base for this stems from the work of Vygotsky (1979), who proposes that the experiences a child has will affect his or her development. The acquisition of spatial understanding is not wholly dependent on some kind of pre-programmed reality but is rather a consequence of a range of social experiences. Teachers play a key role in providing these experiences and in helping children to make sense of them in social contexts. It is vital that we do not underestimate children's ability to respond. Part of this social context is concerned with how teachers construct and deliver the curriculum within the framework provided by the National Curriculum and guidelines. The extent to which children develop spatial understandings is arguably a result of this process.

Integration of geographical skill, place and theme

This leads to a second key principle: the skilful integration of geographical skill, place and theme (Wiegand 1993). This is important because the successful integration of these elements creates a rich context for learning. Geographical skills are not best developed in isolation. Children need to learn the skills of geographical enquiry (for example map skills, questioning skills) in a meaningful way. Place is one key part of this context, whether this is taken to mean the study of an individual classroom, aspects of the school grounds, the area immediately beyond the school or a more distant locality. Themes such as environmental geography, the study of rivers and elements of the human environment provide a second key part of the context and give focus to geography education. This chapter's case study provides an example of how a range of practitioners working with very young children linked a theme on the environment to the development of early map skills within the context of a study focusing on the area within and immediately surrounding the school.

Spiralling skills and concepts

A third principle involves the notion that key concepts should be revisited in more complex forms. If children are exploring the environment immediately beyond the school, they will need to do this in a variety of ways. It will be possible, for example, to map this environment at different levels of complexity. This idea derives from the work of Jerome Bruner and is called a spiral curriculum (see p. 177). It is possible to focus on the same topic or area but study elements of this topic at greater depth and range. In the case study the notion of a spiral curriculum is, as we shall see, definitely present; although the local environment is studied in different ways the progression in map skills, for example, is clearly evident.

THE CASE STUDY

St Mark's playgroup: exploring the local environment

Children aged from under three to seven explored elements of the environment within and immediately beyond the school and playgroup. The environment theme was divided into four areas: homes, local buildings, transport and nature. In 'homes' the children experienced a range of activities, for instance washing up and cleaning pots and pans, to encourage the use of language and identify things we do around the home. Other activities included talking about homes, introducing vocabulary such as 'doors' and 'windows', and encouraging the children to draw and colour pictures. These ideas were reinforced through discussion and story. Similar activities occurred in relation to other environmental features, as with the identification of different forms of transport and the creation of paintings of cars, with the children choosing what colours they should be. Much of the learning focused on generic skills and knowledge related to colour, fine-motor skills, number recognition and social skills.

The older children in the day nursery undertook related activities which developed the 'environment' theme. Environmental jigsaws of street scenes were completed and the resulting conversation led the children to relate this to their own local area. They made a collage of a house and were encouraged to stick on various shapes representing doors and windows. They listened to a tape of environmental sounds and were asked to place a counter on the card bearing the 'picture' of a particular sound. They coloured in a street scene showing different buildings and talked about this with adults on a one-to-one basis. All these activities were designed to develop the children's awareness of their local area, to provide them with geographical vocabulary and early skills of representation.

The reception class: a walk to the park

Jill Reeve worked with the children on a theme centred on a journey to the local park. They walked there discussing features along the way and using a digital camera to take photographs. Back in the classroom the children's photographs were transferred to an interactive whiteboard (or SMART board notebook). This provided a high-quality resource with plenty of opportunity for all the children to view the main features of the walk. The ensuing lesson had a key objective that was closely related to one of the early learning goals for a sense of place: 'To find out about and identify features in the natural environment'. Jill Reeve showed the children the first photograph, which was of the class before the walk: in it the children are sitting on the carpet with their coats on. She then asked them what the photograph was about and scribed their response on the interactive whiteboard below the photograph. Key questions were then asked as a series of digital photographs were displayed. These questions focused on the sequence of events: 'What did we do first?', 'What did we pass next?', 'What else did we see?', 'What did the weather look like?' Because individual children had taken the photographs they were able to remember the correct sequence and build up a complete picture of the walk. As each photograph was shown Jill Reeve scribed the children's description under it. During this time of whole-class discussion a great deal of geographical language emerged, particularly positional language such as 'We went up the hill' and 'We walked past the school'. The children were encouraged to talk about features they remembered but which were not included in the photographs.

The children had created a record of the sequence of the journey, starting at school, walking to and through the local park, noting features on the way, passing the local high school and ending up back in the classroom. Jill Reeve then typed the handwritten scribing onto each digital photograph and made an electronic book together with a hard-copy book of the journey.

Children used this whole-class discussion and activity to prepare, in small groups over a period of time, their own 'maps' of the journey by drawing what they had passed on the way to the park. Each child was asked to draw three things, and the photographs were made available. The children's response to this activity differed markedly. Roy, for example, drew a tree with two leaves, the high school and the football pitch, using a goal posts symbol to represent the last item. His pictures were also in the correct sequence, while those of others had a more random arrangement: 'the park', 'the hill', 'the tree'. While most of the children drew picture maps, there were some interesting representations of the environmental features which demonstrated that some children were developing an understanding of perspective.

At the end of this lesson, the richness of the teaching environment for early geography became apparent. After they had cleared up, the class again gathered on the carpet and took part in further geographical discussion focusing on the magnetic weather board. Children were asked whether they could find the symbol for cloud, and further probing encouraged them to be precise about choosing cloud and not rain! They were also required to select clothes for the magnetic teddy that related to the weather conditions. The conclusion of the lesson involved sharing the story of *Harry's Home* (Anholt and Anholt 1999), in which Harry lives in a city and goes on a journey to her grandfather's house.

Year 1: the playground

An exploration of the work undertaken in Year 1 shows how elements of the work in the reception class were taken further and deepened. As part of a wider theme entitled 'Around and about school: people who help us', the class undertook some work centred on the garden area of the school playground. There were specific objectives, related to statements 4a, 1b, 2e and 3a in the geography section of Curriculum 2000:

- To observe and record the features and layout of the playground.
- To express their own views about their environment and communicate their opinions and ideas in different ways.
- To consider how their environment can be improved.

A series of activities related to the first objective demonstrated clear steps in working towards the production of an individual map showing symbols for features in the school garden and also depicting their relative position. This began with the taking of photographs and moved on to the creation of a human map on site, a whole-class record of this, and finally individual maps.

Prior to this lesson, the class teacher, Yasmeen Hanifa, had taken pictures of it using a digital camera. Before going out to the garden, the children sat in a circle and were shown the photographs. Then Yasmeen asked them where the photographs had been taken. She explained that they were going to go outside to match the photographs to specific places. The children were asked to describe the location of their pictures. Jodie said, 'The plants are in front of the wall.' Once in the garden, the children were asked to stand by the feature in their picture. When the children had become familiar with the pictures and the garden, Yasmeen worked with them to create a 'positional map'. The children gathered in a small area in which three benches form a horseshoe boundary; then each held his or her picture of the garden feature while standing in the correct place relevant to the other children's pictures. In this way they created a human map. Here, it is interesting to observe the children's understandings. One child, Wasimi, understood the need for space between the picture representing the log pile and the one of the flower tubs. Another child suggested that the children holding the pictures of the log pile and the flower tubs should move slightly further apart.

Once the human map was completed the relative position of the features of the garden were reinforced. The ensuing conversation built on their understanding of the relationship between the actual garden and their representation of it.

Back in the classroom, the children created a map of the garden as a whole class. This was done through a series of questions. Yasmeen drew the map by positioning photographs on a sheet of paper. Key questions included 'What did we see first?', 'What did we see next?', 'What did we see at the bottom of the path?' and 'What was along the road fence?' The focus of the discussion moved from teacher to pupil, then from pupil to pupil as children talked among themselves about the relative positions of the photographs.

All this work was finally consolidated in a second session when the children drew individual maps showing the location of various features in the school garden. There was also further discussion at individual and whole-class level, focusing on plan drawing. This was then expressed in individual children's maps that show early use of symbols to depict features in the garden. Roomana's drawing (Figure 3.4) demonstrates a symbolic representation of the tubs and benches.

Year 2: representing journeys, real and imaginary

The Year 1 work on the school grounds was concerned with a gradual movement from the visual to the imagined, from a practical experience to abstract representation from memory. This trend continued in the Year 2 work, where there was an enhanced emphasis on the representation of journeys from imagination. Here there are three key elements:

- Further exploration of the local area using aerial photographs and plans;
- Drawing a map based on a route in a children's story and introducing the idea of symbols;
- Drawing a journey to school.

The journey in the *Funnybones* story was intertwined with the children's understanding that their own maps and symbols represented aspects of their local area. Background work was undertaken using aerial photographs of the

Name: Roo Maha-   November 01

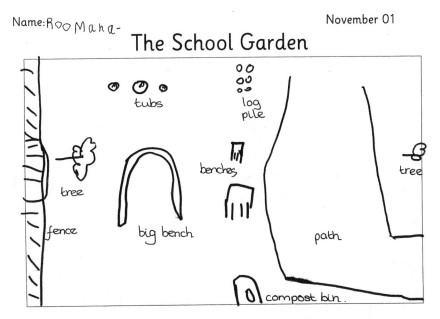

The School Garden

Figure 3.4 (Year 1) Roomana's drawing shows symbolic representation of tubs in the school garden (Learning objective: to draw a simple map of a familiar environment).

school and immediate area that were tied in with large-scale local maps and plans. Various different scales were used as the children identified key local features on both the maps and the aerial photographs.

This activity led to a further exploration of the environment surrounding the school in which the children were encouraged to comment on environmental change in terms of likes and dislikes. There was an introduction to land use as children were asked to draw or write about building features and land features, and to record any changes using the maps and the photographs. Zibya's work (Figure 3.5) demonstrates his understanding of the distinction between buildings and land, and of changes that have occurred.

The next phase of the children's work involved the use of the *Funnybones* story (Ahlberg 2000) to develop an understanding of symbols through the depiction of the route in the story. Finally all this work was brought together as the children prepared their own directional maps from home to school. At the end of this work, it was envisaged that children would have met a number of specific objectives, including:

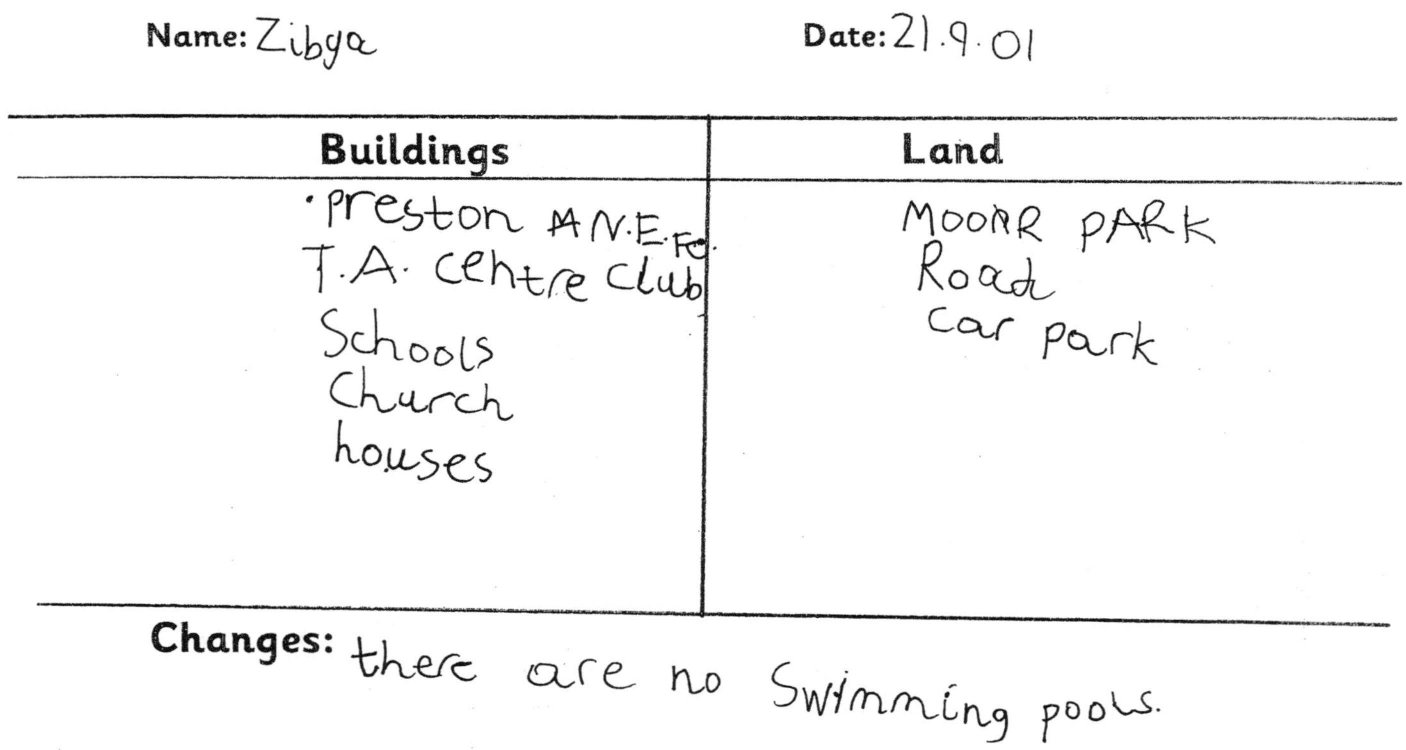

Name: Zibya

Date: 21.9.01

Buildings	Land
· Preston A.N.E.R T.A. centre club Schools Church houses	MOORR PARK Road car park

Changes: there are no swimming pools.

Figure 3.5 Zibya (Year 1) understands the distinction between buildings and land and identifies changes which have occurred (Learning objective: to name features seen locally; to identify any changes that are taking place).

- The ability to use aerial photographs and related plans to recognize local features;
- The ability to make maps for a fictional journey using pictures, symbols and keys;
- The ability to make maps concerned with the locality using pictures, symbols and keys.

ANALYSING THE CHILDREN'S EXPERIENCES

In the first section I outlined three key principles of geographical education in the Early Years: the importance of continually building on key skills and concepts; of integrating skills, theme and place; and of high expectations. The second section described children's experiences of learning geography through a theme centred on the environment. Let us revisit the three principles we established and explore how they were expressed in the classroom work.

The spiral curriculum

In the spiral curriculum, key skills and understandings are revisited in greater depth as time elapses. In analysing this notion, it is appropriate to consider the juxtaposition between the spiral curriculum and the development of map skills. Waters (1998) identifies discrete aspects of map skills such as location, representation, distance, perspective, style, drawing, map use and map knowledge. For each aspect he shows elements of progression in learning from the Foundation Stage to the end of Key Stage 1. In representation, for example, children in reception could be expected to use their own symbols on imaginary maps, while towards the top of Key Stage 1 pupils would use agreed class symbols on simple maps. In the case study some of the reception children were able to develop their own symbols for objects encountered during their local walk while others used pictorial representation. The Year 2 work, by contrast, involved a key objective which focused on the keys and symbols used in the development of a map showing the children's route to school. The concept of representation had been revisited but at greater depth and with more precision with the older children.

Integration

The integration of theme, skill and place was the second principle, and this could also be seen in all the work carried out by the children. In the nursery the children each made a pictorial representation (skill) of their own home (place) and considered elements of the wider local area, through the environmental jigsaws (theme). In the Year 1 class, the school garden (place) was mapped (skill), and later the children were asked to express their likes and dislikes concerning that particular environment (theme). This was replicated in Year 2, where the focus was the wider local area, but again elements of map skills were explored and the children's environmental preferences sought. This linking of theme, skill and place is embedded within both the early learning goals and the Key Stage 1 National Curriculum for geography. The two early learning goals (ELGs) for a sense of place are:

> Observe, find out about and identify features in the place they live and the natural world ... and ... [f]ind out about their environment and talk about those features they like and dislike.
>
> (DFEE/QCA: 2000a)

The first ELG contains strong elements of enquiry skills and a sense of place, while the second has a theme of environmental analysis. The relationship between the three strands is even more pronounced in Key Stage 1, where the geography orders explicitly identify geographical enquiry and skills, a knowledge and understanding of places, and then a knowledge and understanding of patterns and processes, environmental change and sustainable development.

Great expectations

The fundamental principle established in the early part of the chapter can be represented as not underestimating what young children are capable of achieving in geography. In exploring the work that the children did it became apparent that the following had been achieved:

- Talking about our homes and their distinctive identities (nursery);
- Knowing about different forms of transport (nursery);
- Identifying environmental noises and relating these to pictures (nursery);
- Completing a jig map of a local environment (nursery);
- Being able to sequence a journey through the local area by ordering a series of photographs (reception);
- Recalling from memory additional objects in between the photographs (reception);
- Using locational language to describe the places in the photographs (reception);
- Drawing a picture map, and in some cases using symbols as part of this (reception);
- Understanding the relative positions of different objects in the school garden (Year 1);
- Representing the school garden at different scales (Year 1);

- Drawing a simple map of the school garden using some elements of plan view (Year 1);
- Understanding how aerial views relate to maps of the local area (Year 2);
- Knowing how to use this information to identify changes in the local area (Year 2);
- Being able to draw a map from a story (Year 2);
- Drawing a map of the route to school using some common symbols (Year 2).

The principle concerned with understanding the potential for geographical achievement in young children also stressed the importance of the learning context if this is to occur. It is right therefore to conclude by stating that all of the above occurred through the skilful intervention of practitioners in classrooms, both at the planning stage and in the development of actual activities. In an age where all too often the education glass is seen as half full, from time to time it does us good to remind ourselves of children's achievements which have occurred as a result of teachers' expertise.

IDEAS TO FOLLOW UP

Consider a class you have taught in relation to one or two of the main elements of map skills: location, representation, distance, perspective, scale. For each element choose two children who represent the extremes of the ability range and jot down three things they are able either to understand or do in relation to this element. Celebrate their achievement!

SUGGESTIONS FOR FURTHER READING

Palmer, J. (1994) *Geography in the Early Years*, London: Routledge.
    This book provides a fascinating insight into processes of early geographical learning. It is vividly illustrated. Joy Palmer captures the essence of good teaching in Early Years geography.
Conway, D. and Pointon, P. (1996) '"If the world is turning round, how come the piece I'm standing on is flat?" – Early Years geography' in D. Whitebread (ed.), *Teaching and Learning in the Early Years*, London: Routledge.
    This chapter links Early Years geographical theory with practical examples.

BIBLIOGRAPHY

Ahlberg, A. (2000) *Funnybones*, London: Heinemann.
Anholt, C. and Anholt, L. (1999) *Harry's Home*, London: Orchard.

Halocha, J. (1998) *Co-ordinating Geography Across the Primary School*, London: Falmer Press.

Piaget, J. (1954) *The Construction of Reality in the Child*, New York: Basic Books.

Piaget, J. and Inhelder, B. (1956) *The Child's Conception of Space*, London: Kegan Paul.

Piaget, J., Inhelder, B. and Szeminska, A. (1960) *The Child's Conception of Geometry*, London: Routledge & Kegan Paul.

Palmer, J. (1994) *Geography in the Early Years*, London: Routledge.

Scoffham, S. (1998) 'Young geographers' in R. Carter (ed.), *Handbook of Primary Geography*, London: Geographical Association.

Vygotsky, L.S. (1979) *Mind and Society*, Cambridge, MA: Harvard University Press.

Waters, A. (1998) 'Progression and differentiation' in R. Carter (ed.), *Handbook of Primary Geography*, Sheffield: Geographical Association.

Wiegand, P. (1992) *Place in the Primary School*, London: Falmer Press.

Wiegand, P. (1993) *Children and Primary Geography*, London: Cassell.

Chapter 13

Physical development into physical education: is it fair play?

Jim Lavin

In the *Curriculum Guidance for the Foundation Stage* (DFEE/QCA 2000) physical development is described as the improvement of the skills of coordination, control, manipulation and movement. These aspects help children to gain confidence in what they can do and feel the positive benefits of being active and healthy.

The guidance provides clear principles. Practitioners are asked to plan activities which offer appropriate physical challenges using a range of equipment. The children should be given plenty of time to explore, experiment and refine movements and actions. Such opportunities should be regular and frequent. These need to take place in a safe, well-planned and resourced learning environment.

Children should be encouraged to develop skills that promote confidence and independence. Given the opportunity, they will respond to a range of stimuli for movement such as action rhymes, stories, music and props. They should be introduced to the vocabulary of movement. Manipulation and coordination abilities can be encouraged through allowing them the use of both large and small body movements.

However, the National Curriculum for Physical Education (NCPE) provides a different model. Here, the following aspects are delineated: acquiring and developing skills; selecting and applying skills; tactics and compositional ideas; evaluating and improving performance; and knowledge and understanding of fitness and health. This model splits physical education into three subjects: dance, games and gymnastics. Schools can also choose to teach swimming during Key Stage 1.

The debate concerning the type of activity to be offered to children aged from three to eight is informed by a number of researchers. Bilton (2000) made an important distinction between movement and physical development. Physical development (PD) is only one component of movement, which also includes constructive or creative play. Movement is a mode through which children can learn. Manners and Carroll (2000) provide a set of principles for the physical education (PE) of those between the ages of three and seven. Many of these are similar to the Foundation Stage constructs, but they also include the principle that PE builds on what the child can already do. The authors felt that the basic actions of rolling, rocking, climbing, running, jumping, swinging and throwing had already been explored by the time children started school.

The route from free play to structured play is well charted by researchers such as Wetton (1991) and Thomas *et al.* (1988). In this model, children learn about their movement capabilities by selecting their own play activities. Children are allowed to move from one activity to another as they choose. At a point determined by the practitioner, this interest in movement challenges is channelled into a particular learning process. In this process structured play can be defined as play that is teacher-directed. This is goal-oriented and can be planned for either an individual or a group of children.

This chapter examines actual practice in physical development/physical education in a variety of educational settings with the three-to-seven age group, focusing on the following aspects:

- The environment or setting in which physical development/physical education takes place;
- The time given to physical development/physical education;
- The ways in which the Foundation Stage and Key Stage 1 relate to each other.

This chapter is based on video recordings of children undertaking physical play activities in the playgroup at St Mark's day care unit and observation of PE in reception, Year 1 and Year 2 classes at Market Gates Infants' School. In addition, the way children used their time during break and lunch time was analysed, and other practitioners were interviewed.

ST MARK'S PLAYGROUP

The children are provided with play activities within the classroom and, at times determined by the practitioners they are also allowed to use the indoor and the outdoor play areas. The amount of time for play was determined by a number of factors. There were times when the indoor play area was not available. The outdoor play area was used when the weather allowed, and this use rose dramatically during the summer, when the children spent most afternoons outside. There was a good range of activities available to them, but limited amount of space available at the nursery meant that this was not on the same scale as at Market Gates Infants.

The small games equipment included beanbags, bats, variously sized balls and even a basketball ring. Garry Groves and Bindi Patel, two of the playgroup leaders, joined in the children's play, encouraging them to practise their skills and making suggestions about how to get better at throwing and catching; 'travelling with', sending and receiving. The area of physical development was seen as one of the strands of the topic-based approach adopted by the nursery. It was linked to the theme of exploring the environment through a focus on spatial awareness and self-expression: walking, stopping, running to places, moving to music tapes and using the larger outdoor play equipment.

Each child in the nursery had a development chart. One section of this dealt with mobility and large motor skills, including the following:

- throw a ball to an adult standing 2 metres away;
- perform a forward somersault;
- catch a large ball with two hands;
- pedal and steer a bike;
- bounce then catch a ball;
- throw a ball then catch it;
- skip without a rope;
- catch a beanbag with one hand.

Other sections dealt with coordination and manipulation tasks involving finger rhymes and handling objects.

The children were assessed every six months on their progress, which was noted on their chart. It was clear from observing them that they handled and explored the equipment with confidence and assurance, and were happy to experiment and use the equipment in different ways.

THE ENVIRONMENT AS A SETTING FOR PHYSICAL DEVELOPMENT/PHYSICAL EDUCATION

The video-recorded sessions in Market Gates Infants' School provided an opportunity to trace the ways in which the environment was used for physical development and physical education from the nursery and reception through to Years 1 and 2. The Foundation Stage and Key Stage 1 environments within which physical learning took place differed greatly. In the nursery class, some of the physical development activities took place within the classroom itself and the classroom was set out to allow for this: for example, a range of small objects was set out for the children to handle. The teachers, Jane Pick and Mary Gallagher, explained they used the classroom to offer a range of stimuli for movement such as action rhymes, stories and music. Jane said:

We play music in the classroom and we do link the music to movement. They can move as they want with free expression. We play music that makes them want to move.

Mary pointed out the circular musical pads they had just acquired. These were placed on the floor and played a note when a child stood on them. Children explored their use, for example by jumping from one to another in an attempt to link notes. The nursery and reception classes shared an enclosed playground which had an extensive range of play equipment and apparatus. Much of this was in a large store set to one side of the playground.

When the children were allowed out during outdoor play activity, the most popular activity was the bikes. There were a variety of these and at least fifteen children were able to play on them at any one time. It was noticeable that the children who did not get a bike at once waited for their opportunity to get one – they were in constant use.

The sand tray was always well attended, and those playing here tended to stay with the activity for quite some time. It was noticeable that they concentrated on this and were not prone to distractions. Several children played with a variety of balls. It was noticeable that the boys kicked the ball around the playground while the girls tended to stand around bouncing and catching it. One boy spent most of the fifteen-minute break running and kicking a ball, displaying a high level of activity not to mention stamina.

There was a piece of large apparatus in the playgroup which consisted of a low metal climbing frame with a tunnel mounted on top. This was not popular with the children and was underused. The reasons for this were unclear, other than it did not offer the range of swinging, sliding, hiding, jumping opportunities that more modern frames do.

Several of the children were engaged in creating and developing games concepts. Two experimented with setting up plastic skittles in different patterns and then hitting them with a ball so that they knocked into each other. The gardening activity was also popular. The children related well to their adult supervisors, who encouraged play. The children also related well to each other and there were no signs of conflict.

In the Year 1 and Year 2 playground the children were again supplied with a wide range of apparatus. Susmita Weaver was organizing a skipping activity, which was very popular. Various wheeled toys were again in demand, ranging from chariots and rickshaws to Pedalows. Many of these presented significant physical challenges to the children, and it was clear that they were very skilled in their use. There was also a wide range of items for imaginative play: one girl was being pulled in a plastic bread tray by a team of children, while others experimented with balls on elastic.

The playground also had a quiet area with a garden in one corner which was fenced off. This was laid out with walkways and wooden garden benches. Here, several children sat quietly reading.

The overall impression was one of activity and enjoyment. There were no tears or arguments; no child went to the adult supervisors complaining about the actions of another. The supervisors were thus able to respond to the children's needs. I noticed one woman supervisor playing football with a child, providing a stereotype-breaking role model.

THE TIME GIVEN TO PHYSICAL DEVELOPMENT/ PHYSICAL EDUCATION

There was a clear delineation in terms of the time given to physical development and physical education. As the children moved through the system they were given less time in which to be physically active. At the Foundation Stage, physical development is a major component of the children's learning experiences. The *Curriculum Guidance for the Foundation Stage* (2000) identifies it as one of the six areas of learning.

The evidence gained from this case study supports the claim that aspects of physical development account for at least a third of the children's time while in the nursery and reception classes. This takes into account the time spent with 'small world' toys, construction sets and sand and water trays, time which can even be increased during the summer term when the children are encouraged to spend more time on outdoor play activities. Even time spent putting on coats and other clothing can be seen as contributing to their physical development.

The amount of time allowed was greatly curtailed in Years 1 and 2. This disparity is partly explained by the move to the National Curriculum Physical Education guidelines, which encompass games, gymnastic and dance activities but exclude the manipulative and fine motor skills involved in such activities as cutting, gluing, painting, model-making and so on. In this study, the time spent at Key Stage 1 on physical education was only two lessons a week. Lesley Craig, a Year 1 teacher, pointed out the difference from the Foundation Stage:

> We get two sessions, which is a lot different from when I taught in reception, because we would get the physical education sessions plus two outside play sessions – so it's quite a big difference.

That noted, the two sessions a week given to physical education were used well. The children were kept active throughout the lessons and were challenged in terms of their movement capabilities.

The subject leader for physical education, Patsy Roebuck, explained that the teachers were very positive about the value and benefits of PE for the children. However, the pressures on curriculum time caused by the introduction of literacy and numeracy hours meant that less time was available for Foundation subjects such as PE.

THE RELATIONSHIP BETWEEN THE FOUNDATION STAGE AND THE NATIONAL CURRICULUM FOR PHYSICAL EDUCATION

The research identified a number of issues relating to this interface. The characteristics of each are presented below. This illustrates the difference in emphasis between the Foundation Stage guidance on physical development and the Key Stage 1 curriculum for physical education.

Foundation Stage physical development			National Curriculum physical education: Key Stage 1		
Play-centred	Exploration	Experimentation	Skill focus	Teacher-directed	Subject-based
Wide range of equipment	Creativity	Autonomy	Developing, selecting and applying skills	Limited equipment/ apparatus	Cooperative working
Manipulation	Coordination	Confidence	Exercise and health notions	Compositional ideas	Evaluate and improve performance
Increasing control	Respond to rhythm, safety music, story	Understanding	Watching and listening	Express feelings through movement	Remember and repeat simple skills and actions

It is possible to view these very different models as providing a tension between the Foundation Stage and Key Stage 1. Are children denied the opportunity to express themselves freely at Key Stage 1? Do some children need to have the physical development model continued into Years 1 and 2 in order to develop appropriately? Do we stop them 'playing' in the physical sense too early?

The video record of PE lessons in Years 1 and 2 provided a very different version of learning through the physical from the playgroup, nursery and reception class videos. Both the teachers, Helen Bawtry and Nick Salmon, were experienced practitioners with a belief in the value of PE; indeed, Helen is a PE specialist and a very effective subject leader for it in the school. The lessons themselves were models of good practice. There was a clear focus to the learning; the children were interested and challenged by the learning tasks, and responded well to them. There was a quiet atmosphere of purposeful endeavour pervading the lessons, all very different from the free-flowing, free-expression kind of physical activity the children undertook in the playground at break and lunch times. The lessons themselves were part of an overall scheme of work which Helen had developed. This provided for differentiation and progression over the Key Stage.

That noted, there was debate about the level of expectation placed on the children. Nick Salmon, who teaches Year 1, described how a boy named Ricky often found it difficult to respond to instructions: 'Ricky is another little boy who just stands there, unless he partners someone. Then he will hold someone's hand and just walk around. He will not join in.' I wondered whether he could understand Nick's instructions. 'Oh, yes', Nick said, 'he understands the instructions. I don't know what it is. He will just stand there.'

One could speculate whether, for this child, the 'formal' lesson setting for PE is something he is not able to cope with. However, there was the flexibility for certain children to have continued access to play activities. I asked Helen Bawtry if she thought that maybe we stopped children playing too early, and she replied:

> This is a personal view, but I think, sometimes, yes, with certain children. There are some very able children in my class who would get nothing from free expression, from unfocused lessons. But there are certain children who would benefit from more play activity.

This study has shown a significant difference in the learning of children as they move from the age three to seven in terms of their physical experience. The physical development aspect of the Foundation Stage guidance deals with generic concepts of movement and includes areas that disappear at Key Stage 1: for example, such activities as the use of 'small world' toys, riding bikes, playing in the sandpit and gardening. Children also spend less time on physical activity at Key Stage 1. One could argue that their physical education curriculum is impoverished because of this. The views and practice of teachers also influence the nature and range of physical experiences presented to children at Key Stage 1. The existence of an exceptional subject leader for PE, such as Patsy Roebuck, can have a profound effect on the quality of children's learning experiences. The case for 'super-teachers' to share their experience and expertise with other schools is strong.

CONCLUSION

This small study showed how free play and structured play act as building blocks for the development of physical skills and creative activity. Overall, the views of the teachers involved was that whilst there may be some tensions, the National Curriculum for physical education provides a necessary progression from the physical development aspect of the Foundation Stage to the more structured learning at Key Stage 1.

BIBLIOGRAPHY

Bilton, H. (2000) *Outdoor Play in the Early Years: Management and Innovation*, London: Fulton.

Hopper, B., Grey, J. and Maude, T. (2000) *Teaching Physical Education in the Primary School*, London: Falmer.

Manners, H.K. and Carroll, M.E. (2000) *A Framework for Physical Education in the Early Years*, London: Falmer.

Thomas, J.R., Lee, A.M. and Thomas, K.T. (1988) *Physical Education for Children: Concepts into Practice*, Champaign, IL: Human Kinetics.

Totsky Hammett, C. (1992) *Movement Activities for Early Childhood*, Champaign, IL: Human Kinetics.

Wetton, P. (1991) *Physical Education in the Nursery and Infant School*, London: Routledge.

Williams, A. (ed.) (2000) *Primary School Physical Education Research into Practice*, London: RoutledgeFalmer.

Chapter 14

Numeracy all around: developing children's mathematics through role play and directed daily experience

Margaret Foster and Robin Foster

> Children's mathematical development arises out of daily experiences in a rich interesting environment.
>
> (DFEE/QCA 2000)

The use of role play and directed daily experience in the planning of work at the Foundation Stage and Key Stage 1 are seen as being important. There is ample evidence to suggest that effective learning in the Early Years is based on children's experiences. The exploration offered by play and structured directed tasks allows children to learn naturally. Jane Drake (2001: 61) emphasizes the need for this structure to be part of the planning process:

> An effective early years curriculum recognises the need for children to be 'active learners'. Through interacting with, and responding to, the world around them, children acquire skills and knowledge and develop concepts. Well-planned provision in the early years environment will offer them a wealth of exciting opportunities for exploration and investigation.

Lise Elliot (1999: 414) sees children of about four years old as being particularly able to learn from role play, as they are able to appreciate for themselves the way in which they are beginning to know how to adopt another's view of the world:

> You can see this in their play when they adopt the perspective of different roles – mother, child, doctor, patient, friend – and begin assigning people's actions to internal motives, wishes, secrets and the like.

The adoption of the Literacy and Numeracy Strategies at Key Stage 1 might suggest that there is less demand for role play and thematic planning for English and mathematics. In the work undertaken for this study it was found that even though the school was following the Numeracy Strategy for the daily mathematics lesson, there was significant planning for mathematics still going on in the context of role play and in work arranged as part of wider themes in other parts of the school day.

OUTLINE OF STUDY

Market Gates is a large urban first school with a varied ethnic mix. The work was carried out over a month during which the children and their teachers were observed as they carried out their mathematics lessons. In the school there was evidence of the way a rich and interesting environment had a direct link to the quality of mathematical learning. Its staff members were committed to careful planning of the experience for children in an integrated and focused way. This was especially noticeable as children, parents and visitors entered the school. Three aspects of the school's approach to the teaching of mathematics were selected for observation:

1   *Whole-school ethos.* One feature of the school was the way in which planning was dealt with. There was a whole-school ethos where Early Years practitioners worked and planned together to create an environment which offered opportunities for acquiring mathematics. Lessons, displays, resources and activities were planned with an emphasis on creating a context for the learning of mathematics. Staff from the school also liaised with other Early Years providers, including those from St Mark's day care centre, in the planning of the work.

2   *Role play.* The use of role play was an integral feature of the planning and organization in the school. This was achieved by arranging carefully timetabled sessions for it during the school day. The planning for the reception class explicitly addressed the role-play requirements. The work for Year 1 and Year 2 children was based on the main theme but also allowed opportunities for the use of equipment and apparatus in expressive ways. Two areas – one a former hall and the other a classroom – were set aside especially for role play.

3   *Designated rooms and display.* Mathematics is taught in one of three rooms reserved exclusively for that purpose. Each of these dedicated rooms also serves as a class base for individual groups of children. The particular rooms used for the teaching and learning of mathematics have a specific mathematics 'feel', with all the displays and equipment in them being related to the subject. The children begin and end their day in their own class base, but each year group has access to specialist rooms. For each year group one room each is available for literacy and another for numeracy; a third room is equipped for science, art, design and

technology, and a fourth caters for role-play sessions. Display was an integral part of the planning process and the different rooms reflected the subjects taught in them.

Whole-school ethos

Teachers and practitioners plan together on a regular basis. The themes for the sessions are arranged in advance in such a way that every term children have opportunities for covering a balanced selection of the curriculum. Over each school year a wide range of subjects is selected. The theme for the autumn term was 'Our environment: around and about'. This allowed for a strong focus on the environment and geography. The planned topic for the spring term was 'Communication', allowing for the development of English, particularly as many of the children spoke it as a second language. The third term's focus was 'The living world', which afforded opportunities to explore science topics. Mathematics was explored throughout wherever opportunities arose. The overall intention was to use the children's own experience of interaction with others and their immediate environment.

Each class had its daily mathematics lesson with its own teacher in one of the mathematics rooms. Typically, the oral mental starter was undertaken with all the children sitting on the carpet. The main part of the lesson made use of the entire room, which had been carefully prepared before the children arrived so there was efficient transition between the parts of the lesson. The planning for the daily mathematics lesson was carried out using an A3 format for the weekly plan allowing for differentiated work for four different groups defined by their needs.

The numeracy lessons followed the threefold structure, but the main section of the lesson had the class working in four differentiated bands. In Year 1, one of the activities involved a number trail outside the classroom. The children were supervised by a trainee teacher who encouraged them to complete the activity which involved the counting and ordering of selected objects in the school environment.

As part of the project we visited St Mark's day care centre playgroup. Children talked about mathematics in their indoor and outdoor play activities. The staff created a climate that focused on encouraging the children to feel peaceful and explore the opportunities of a rich environment. The play and daily activities were planned so that they had a range of opportunities for mathematical exploration. A wall display of snowmen gave the stimulus for a discussion on number, embedded in a lively context. One occasion we especially enjoyed was when the children ate a meal together. During this time they talked and explored mathematical language in a relaxed and real-life atmosphere. The adult–child interaction was of a high quality.

Integrating mathematics into the main theme

In school the teachers and other practitioners planned the work in the role-play areas and activities based on the main theme in advance. The equipment and activities were chosen carefully to relate to the main theme, and adults working in the areas were able to respond to the children's needs as the session progressed. The teachers planned for various curriculum areas in the their weekly plans. The mathematical aspects of the planning have been extracted for the following tables:

An example of teacher planning from reception

Predicting	When looking at the patterns that are found around the school: *What comes next?*
Sequencing	Numbers. *For example:* 1–8 in the X-ray department (role play).
Ordering	As above
Number	Counting: Count 1–5, then to 10. In role play count groups of mobile phones, purses and shoes. These can be checked at the end of the session.
Shape	Focus on 'circle', 'triangle', 'square', 'cone' and 'sphere'. *Can we find these around the school?* Using a book made up of photographs of places within and outside the school, the children identify a place, then check by looking at the actual place.
Language	Encourage talk to include the vocabulary and ideas in each of the sections above.

Example of teacher planning from Year 2

Predicting	Number sequences. *What number comes next?*
Sequencing	Repeating patterns, translation.
Ordering	Odd and even numbers, door numbers, patterns of five.
Number	Multiplication: vehicles with two wheels, four wheels, etc.
Shape	Shapes in the environment. Two-dimensions: seen on houses. Three-dimensions: symmetrical shapes. Patterns.
Language	Shape, side, corner, faces.
Handling data	Traffic survey, block graph, pictogram. *How many? How many more than?*

Role play

When planning for the work in the school, all the staff met regularly to chart out what was happening in the role-play areas as well as arranging the work for the numeracy sessions. In each of the role-play areas there was a member of staff responsible for organizing the sessions for the children.

With the reception class, the role play took place in the large room that was set out with a home corner, a hospital and a hospital canteen. This provided many opportunities for the use of mathematical language. An interesting use was made of the telephone: the teachers pre-programmed it to give a recorded message which was only heard when a child typed the sequence 1–2–3–4–5–6. The hospital role-play area offered many opportunities for mathematical language. There was an X-ray machine and children were encouraged to talk about it. Waiting room numbers were introduced to encourage sequencing and queuing. The adults in the area engaged the children in talking about what they were doing and mathematical language was developed.

The Year 2 focus for role play was money. They had a doctor's surgery, a chemist's and a bank. The staff focused their questioning on the exchange of money in the bank and chemist's shop. Discussion on temperature, weight and height was encouraged in the doctor's surgery.

Designated rooms and display

Another significant feature of the school and its planning was the use of display. As with the numeracy session and the role-play activities, it was planned by the whole staff in keeping with the overall structure of the curriculum. The displays were of children's work and were of a type that encouraged the children to interact with them. They offered a celebration of the children's personal achievements as well as allowing them to touch, rearrange and be involved with them.

The way in which the various elements of the planning and activity were integrated with one another was demonstrated in the production of displays. One such display is indicative of this integration. In preparing a display on 'shape' the mathematical theme was evident, but other features were noted. Teachers working cooperatively planned its creation, with children contributing both ideas and material. The reception class supplied work on squares, with a colour theme of blue. The Year 1 class contributed triangles with a linked colour theme of pink and red; the display included aspects of shading. The Year 2 children's mathematics focus was on circles, which were displayed using a range of fabrics. In addition, the Year 2 children designed wallpaper, which also became part of the display, but they also integrated this into role play for themselves and the reception class. The Year 2 children took wallpaper samples to show to the reception children; they then measured the space where the wallpaper was going to be displayed. The reception children voted for their choice of wallpaper, and the results were tallied. Once chosen by reception children, it was this paper that was delivered in the correct quantity and hung on the wall. In this way many mathematical ideas were practised and explored. The finished product was not just evidence of the teachers' planning but also the result of children working with each other and teachers to produce something of which they were all justifiably proud.

One particularly stylistic aspect of the display is worthy of note. As indicated above, much of the display involved the children's work. For many of the displays they were encouraged to draw and write with thin black lines on white paper. This was noticeable and eye-catching. The children were keen to show visitors the work and to take pride in their contributions. The children's own labelling using this style was adopted for notices and artefacts in the role-play areas, giving the areas a strong flavour of child ownership.

CONCLUSION

The experience the children had of mathematics comprised the daily mathematics lesson together with many and varied opportunities in role play and in work based on the topic. The ethos and school environment provided the children with opportunities that developed an attitude of motivation on the part of those learning. The well-organized role play gave the children the incentive to explore for themselves and be involved in their own learning. In brief, for much of the day they did what they liked, but at the same time they did what the teacher wanted! In other words, the children were well motivated to interact with the tasks they were presented with, but the teachers and other practitioners had planned the additional experiences so well that the children were fully occupied.

Tricia David (1999: 5) acknowledges this delicate mixture of children's exploration and adult planning:

> Although learning is an interactive process, best facilitated by the appropriate intervention of adults, there are other factors which need to be considered which may affect children's learning. Motivation is one important factor. Activities which stem from the child's interest and therefore produce intrinsic motivation are more likely to lead to effective learning.

In both Market Gates Infants' School and in the playgroup, motivating the children was at the centre of the teaching and learning of mathematics. This took place in a variety of contexts. The designated mathematics rooms were bright and cheerful, with the appropriate equipment to hand. This allowed not only for the daily mathematics lesson to be delivered efficiently, but also for other activities to be developed. The role-play sessions were directed in such a way as to allow the teachers to be confident about what would be learnt, yet they also gave the children ample freedom to become responsible for their own mathematical learning.

GROUP ACTIVITY

If you and your Key Stage 1 colleagues were to use the idea of a vet's surgery to create a role-play area in your reception classroom:

- What would you provide for the children?
- What briefing would you give to parent helpers or Year 11 students on school placement who were going to help in the role-play area you have created?

BIBLIOGRAPHY

Bottle, G. and Alfrey, C (1999) 'Making sense of early mathematics' in T. David (ed.), *Teaching Young Children*, London: Paul Chapman.

David, T. (1999) *Young Children Learning*, London: Paul Chapman.

Drake, J. (2001) *Planning Children's Play and Learning in the Foundation Stage*, London: David Fulton.

Elliot, L. (1999) *Early Intelligence*, London: Penguin.

Griffiths, R. (1988) *Maths Through Play*, London: Macdonald.

Looking back on 'Our environment'

When the staff from St Mark's day care centre and Market Gates Infants' School met college tutors in October 2001 they had identified their hopes for the project on 'Our environment'. Jean Rutter, director of the day care centre, had said that her staff were under constant day-to-day pressure to respond to family crises and that her children's attendance might be spasmodic. For this reason staff were not always able to plan learning activities; parents were often not able to become involved in their children's learning, and many children were too preoccupied to benefit fully from the experiences provided. Jean hoped that the project might help to refocus the playgroup activities more clearly on educational objectives.

Unfortunately we did not have time to return to the day care centre or the school after Christmas, and by that time the manuscript of our book was due at the publisher's. But we were more than delighted to receive the following fax from Jean Rutter:

> I should like to thank all members of the college team; we gained a great deal from the experience. St Mark's staff enjoyed working jointly with the members of the multidisciplinary team and felt that they were able to bounce ideas off them. It also helped us to focus on why we undertake different activities with the children and the importance of early learning structured through play. This is particularly important to us as our primary role and function is seen as offering family support to children who are assessed by the social work team as being 'children in need'.

Anne Dubois, head teacher at Market Gates Infants' School, also found that liaison between her staff and colleagues from St Martin's had been 'a most enriching experience for the school' – and this is a school full of rich experiences.

But when we look back on 'Our environment', the chief beneficiaries were really the college tutors. Time and other constraints had meant that it had not been possible to get to know families in the day care centre, although some college tutors had enjoyed a family lunch time and all had learned a great deal about the work of the centre. They also greatly valued the opportunity to work with the teachers at Market Gates to explore practical issues in real situations. They were clear about the ways in which this benefited their work with students in college, as they explained in the college newsletter:

> Perhaps there is some Darwinian principle at work here, but these Early Years practitioners were all good-natured, dedicated and hard-working, with the best interests of the children at heart; their other defining characteristic was a well-developed sense of humour!

> A stimulating and exciting experience. The difficulty lay in trying to capture in words the atmosphere, where teachers have created such individual environments.

> This was a wonderful opportunity. Apart from being involved in the very positive problem-solving atmosphere, it was extremely helpful to see the way in which teachers were making use of ICT related to history; this experience will be a great asset for my future work with students.

> I enjoyed the opportunity to follow through one of the six areas of learning – physical development – across the age-phases. It's a pity that we can't build this sort of collaboration more into our teaching approaches, into the way we write and teach our courses . . . the problem is always time.

Patsy Roebuck wrote to Jim Lavin to tell him that work on the new playground had just begun: a red zone with a cage for football games; a blue zone for aiming, skipping and throwing; a yellow zone where children could 'chill out' or play table-top games in the garden. 'They will be able to further games skills in informal ways at break and lunch times', Patsy said. That should enhance the continuity in children's experiences and extend the formal PE lessons. Jim will be returning in the summer with his video camera – and his students.

Postscript

At the outset of this project concern was expressed about the possibility that the different curricula in Foundation Stage and Key Stage 1 might make effective and explicit progression difficult. It was also suggested that the differing views of how children learn which are implicit in the National Curriculum and the *Curriculum Guidance for the Foundation Stage* might also be problematic in terms of progression from one stage to the next. The project produced some interesting results and observations. Because of the nature of the research it would be unwise to claim that the study proves that progression does or does not exist. However, the richness of the observations and discussion offers the opportunity for readers to draw their own conclusions.

The authors made some interesting observations as they worked through their individual case studies. Andrea Brook, writing in Part 2, came to the conclusion that 'At all ages, but most especially with young children, the outcomes should be determined by the responses of the children.' This is a sentiment totally in keeping with those expressed by the pioneers of early years education who proposed a child-centred approach to the subject. There is no indication that adopting this position interfered with the development of children's learning in art.

In Part 3, Christine Cooper writes: 'Teachers feel deprofessionalized as they mediate government policy and their own philosophy. This clearly indicates that there is a tension for many teachers between what they believe should take place in primary education and what actually does take place. Regardless of the possible assumptions implicit in both the National Curriculum for Key Stage 1 and the *Curriculum Guidance for the Foundation Stage*, teachers do develop their own philosophy of education and their own beliefs about how children learn best. This informal theory is based on a knowledge of theory tempered in the light of experience. Teaching success will often depend on how well teachers manage and resolve this tension.'

This project was primarily concerned with progression across the Foundation Stage and Key Stage 1. Interestingly, the authors identify a whole range of different types of progression between the two stages. In Part 1,

Owain Evans identifies a progression in children's understanding of design. 'The youngest children were encouraged to be aware of the design potential of what could have been a teacher-dominated activity. In Year 1 they created their own designs for moving pictures and in Year 2 they applied their design and technology skills with confidence.' In Part 2, Nigel Toye, working in the area of drama, found progression in three aspects of his teaching: an increase in understanding as the children grew older, an increase in the length of time the children were able to sustain the drama, and an increase in the number of children capable of being successfully grouped together for the drama. Liz Elliott and Pete Saunders found progression in the sorts of ICT activity with which the children could engage. All age groups were working on the task of retelling a story but different approaches were found to be more appropriate for each age group. In Part 1, Lisa Melbourne and Chris Sixsmith indicate the progression of the skill of exploration from nursery, where exploration is being initiated, to Year 2, where the exploration is moving much more towards investigation. In all areas, progression from the Foundation Stage to Key Stage 1 was identified.

The only area that indicated some significant change from one stage to the next was PE. Jim Lavin reported that there was a significant difference between the PE taught in the Foundation Stage and that taught in Key Stage 1. The work done in the Foundation Stage was not seen as being inappropriate to progression to Key Stage 1 but was seen as being very different. The main contributory factor was felt to be the differing amounts of time available for physical development in the Foundation Stage and PE in Key Stage 1. It was suggested that the significant reduction in the amount of time spent on PE in Key Stage 1 impoverished the subject in that Key Stage.

In Part 3, Neil Simco indicated that in terms of the integration of theme, skill and place there was a clear spiral curriculum. Children met the skills and concepts repeatedly at different levels as they progressed through the two Key Stages. He argued that these basic ideas were embedded in both the National Curriculum and the *Curriculum Guidance for the Foundation Stage*. It seems clear that in each of the three parts of the project, despite the different contexts and curricula, a successful progression does take place between the Foundation Stage and Key Stage 1. It is suggested that it is the common embedded elements in both sets of curricula which allow for this progression. However, what is clear is that the most important factor governing the success of this progression is the skill of the teachers in both Key Stages at interpreting the curriculum in terms of their understanding of both the learning process and the needs of their children.

Afterword

The letters of Edward Lear include a reply to a small girl who wrote to him, many years after the Owl and the Pussy-cat set sail, to ask what eventually happened to them. He tells her that, following the Pussy-cat's unfortunate tree accident some years later, the Owl sailed on with their extensive brood and eventually became beached in Cornwall, where they lived a modestly bohemian life.

Well, we can still be found in the north-west of England, some of us may be just slightly bohemian, and we certainly sighted the land where the Bong-tree grows: where children explore, form, reform and record their worlds through story, art, music and dance.

And if you think that is a tall story, then try and follow the map!

Index